A Kickass Book On Qualitative Research

KUMAR KUNAL JHA

ISBN: 9798720034580

DEDICATION

To all those who lost their lives

To all those who fought at the frontline

To all those who stayed at home and stayed strong

To all those who didn't have a home

To all those who walked miles

CONTENTS

ACKNOWLEDGMENTS

Thank you, Progyaa and Zubaer, for helping me with proofreading, editing and cover design for this book. I would not have been able to do this without you.

Thank you, Maa (Meera Shankar), Pappa (Rajmohan Jha), Vishal and Sasmita Palo ma'am for always believing in me.

Thank you, Lucia, Rohit, Mohan, Prem and Rohan Babu for constant love and support.

Thank you, Debopriyo Bhattacherjee & Martin Karaffa for being such amazing mentors.

Thank you, Tata Institute of Social Sciences, my alma mater, for giving me a safe space where I was able to explore my identity.

Thank you, the Dalai Lama Fellows for introducing me to mindfulness and authentic leadership.

And thank you, to all my students who taught me to be a better qualitative researcher.

CHAPTER 1
INTERPRETATION AND OBSERVATION

In 2015, I had an opportunity to attend a free workshop on 'art-based therapy'. I had little to no clue about what was in store. I was attending the workshop for free food and the conference kit (do not judge, I was a PhD student living on a tight budget and I was drawn to words such as 'free' and 'cheap'). The instructor had completed his master's degree in 'Intermedial Art Therapy', and up until then I was not aware of the existence of such a field or specialisation in art-based therapy (ignorant me!). But as he introduced himself and his work, especially the use of art-based activities in clinical setups and hospitals, I was hooked on to him.

There were 30 people, including me, attending the workshop. After a brief introduction of the instructor, the attendees also introduced themselves. Post that we started with an exercise. The instructor gave us all an A3 paper, some watercolours, and a brush, and gave us the following instruction.

"Using the watercolour, you have to make strokes on the paper. You only have to make strokes. It does not have to mean anything, no form or shape. Keep your wrist relaxed while making these strokes. Focus on your breathing and breathe slowly. Express yourself with these strokes and feel free to use the colours that you like."

Exercise 1.1: 'I am Picasso'

Before reading ahead, follow the above instructions (given to us during the workshop) and complete the exercise. In case you do not have watercolours - take a pen/pencil and paper (any old newspaper would also do) and try doing the exercise for 15 to 20 minutes. Do not make the absence of watercolour or an A3 paper an excuse for skipping the exercise. Make the most of the material you have around you. After completing the exercise, reflect for 5 minutes on how this made you feel. What feeling emerged out of you while doing this exercise? If possible, make a note of these reflections.

After some time, the instructor decided to glance at the participants' works and the way these strokes were coming to life. As soon as he went to the first participant, he had a critical look on his face, which he tried his best to hide. The first participant had made – what seemed like to me from a distance – two mountains and a river flowing between them. The instructor took a deep breath while still looking at the picture (somewhat disappointed) and announced to the class loud and clear.

"Everyone, may I have your attention, please! Please do not make portraits or diagrams. Remember, I told you to let go of any form, shapes, or design while doing this exercise. You are just required to make strokes using the brush. These lines do not have to mean anything. You do not have to draw a picture. Just strokes."

The instructor's disappointment was to only increase with every other attendee. The second student had made a huge ugly smiley face and painted it yellowish-orange. The instructor was not disappointed because the pictures were shabby, but because we failed to follow the basic instruction of letting go of forms, shapes, and designs. How difficult could it have been for a roomful of academicians and PhD scholars to follow these simple instructions? An exercise that was meant to relax us (the participants) had somewhat stressed the instructor.

In case you have done the exercise, what did you do? Were you able to follow the instructions of not giving into drawing forms, design, and shapes, or were you one of the few successful individuals who 'made only strokes'? Irrespective of what you did in the exercise, pause and reflect on what is present for you at the moment.

The intention behind sharing this story/exercise: On a more surface level, this story and the exercise may seem essential for teaching us the importance of listening skills or rather exposing our poor listening skills. That we, humans, generally do not listen well. Most of us are bad listeners. Further, listening is one of the critical skills that any qualitative researcher should have. However, on a deeper level, this story is really about us being social animals that attach meaning to everything. It is difficult for us to not attach meaning to things, behaviours, people, actions, and spaces. We are so used to attaching meaning to things that even when we are asked not to, we either still end up attaching meaning (thanks to our poor listening skills) or we attach meaning to the act/instruction of not attaching meaning to anything (thanks to our ability of metacognitive thinking). Hence, we as humans keep giving/attaching meaning to things. **We interpret things almost all the time –** it is difficult for us to stop attaching meanings (at times, even when we are instructed not to)!

What is interpretation?

Oxford Languages and Google Dictionary define interpretation as 'the action of explaining the meaning of something' and/or as 'an explanation or way of explaining'.

Irrespective of the purpose that interpretation solves, we must always aim to have our interpretations based on 'thick' or detailed observations/descriptions in qualitative research. Hence, one of the primary ways to have better interpretations is to have thick (detailed) observations and descriptions, and use these observations as the foundation to our interpretations. In this chapter, we will strive to understand some of the most important things about interpretation and observation. Further, through practical exercises, we will also improve our observation skills, which will help us become awesome qualitative researchers! By now, we have understood that all humans interpret by attaching meaning to things around us and that we do it all the time, hence, interpretation, as an act or process, is not exclusive to researchers. Social sciences research (both qualitative or quantitative) is not free from the researcher's interpretations. However, how interpretations are treated/seen by qualitative researchers versus quantitative researchers is different. (More on this later in the book)

Fun fact: Did you know that the interpretative method of research is/was interchangeably used by many researchers with the term qualitative research? (More on this in Chapter 2.)

Exercise 1.2: So much in the name!

Let us interpret our names and answer these few questions.

What does your name mean? Why?

What does/did it mean to people who named you? Why?

What does it mean to you? Is your meaning similar/different from the larger cultural meaning of your name? Why?

Does your name have any interesting meaning in popular culture?

E.g.: '*Pappu*', a common name and nickname in northern India, is now used to signify a not smart man or a person who cannot do basic things!

"Pappu can't dance saala", a popular song from a Bollywood movie, *'Jaane Tu Ya Jaane Na'*, signified that *Pappu* cannot even do the basic and simple act of dancing!

Does your name mean anything else in a different culture/language? What? If not, try finding it out.

E.g.: '*Pappu*' in Telugu (a South Indian language) literally translates to lentils.

Okay, some serious questions…

Does your name indicate anything about society or its structure?

Does your name hint at your race, religion, gender, caste, class, profession, recognition (Sir, Padmashree, etc.)   ?

Do you like your name? Why?

If not, then why have you not changed it?

Take some time and reflect on these questions. Write your reflections in the space provided. **Remember the golden rule: 'thick descriptions/observations for better interpretations'.**

I hope that this exercise helped you understand that even something as simple as your name has so much meaning attached to it and tells so much about the structures of the society you live in. Further, the meaning you would associate with your name may be different from those who might have named you, from the meaning in your culture to that in other cultures that you may or may not know.

Now, imagine how things and objects in our surroundings (that are so commonly used in our mundane lives, that we might not even think about them) can tell us so much about the people, their practices, and the larger culture. Before understanding and practising the scientific mode of observation that enables us to have better interpretations, let us first understand more about 'meaning' in the context of qualitative research.

Subjective and Cultural: Subjective Meaning is the meaning attached by an individual. We all have our subjective meanings of the world around us, and they are influenced by our prior experiences, belief systems, and information/knowledge of this world. We might not have knowledge or information about certain realities, but we might still attach meaning to them. For example, during elections, you might come across many voters/individuals who might not even have basic information of the politicians that they might elect, their past work and involvement in politics, the promised manifesto for the future, but these voters/individuals may still have strong opinions about who should win the elections or on their leadership capabilities. I have come across people who did not know simple facts such as who the president and the vice-president of their country are but had strong subjective meanings/opinions attached to the political environment – often based on ignorance, propaganda, misinformation, and the perceived charisma of a few politicians.

To understand ignorance better, we classify it as active and passive ignorance. Active ignorance is when an individual is aware of their lack of awareness but chooses actively to stay away from gaining any further information. In such cases, the individual may think that the information/knowledge they have is enough to form an opinion on certain aspects, or that gaining further information may be mentally draining/depressing. For example, after a few days post the COVID-19 outbreak, I stopped watching the news or actively seeking information on the number of patients or fatalities as it was too depressing and mentally draining. We are also living in a world of information overload, and it is humanly not possible to be aware of all things. Hence, individuals might choose the areas of knowledge/information that they think add higher value in their lives, also a form of active ignorance. Passive ignorance is where the individual is not aware of their non-awareness about certain things. In today's post-truth world, where narratives are easily adulterated and people are exposed continuously to fake news, we may think that the information/knowledge we possess is 'true' even when it might not be. All of us ignore both passively and actively. Further, in the era that we are living in, it is challenging for an individual to be completely aware of all the knowledge in a particular field. This is also the foundation of scientific temperament.

- We do not know everything about anything.
- We cannot be sure what we know will be true always, in all conditions and situations (hence, it is important to keep questioning even the things that we know).

Though there are different schools of thought on how subjectivity should be treated and acknowledged in qualitative research, it is important and given that subjectivity exists in social sciences research. Subjectivity is not a bad thing, but, as qualitative researchers, we should try to be aware of these subjectivities (knowing that we cannot be completely aware of all our subjectivities and biases) and own and celebrate them in the research. A qualitative researcher should state the subjectivities that frame their worldview as it leads to a more scientific way of doing research. In fact, the founding fathers of interpretative/qualitative research have critiqued non-interpretive/positivist or quantitative methods for the manner in which subjectivity has been treated – especially by social sciences researchers who have attempted to replicate the research process from pure sciences. (If you find this difficult to understand, do not worry I have this covered in a more lucid language in the next chapter)

Like you would have your subjective meaning and worldview other individuals will also have theirs. Your meaning of things or the environment around you may be similar or different from theirs. I believe that the meaning given to the world by two researchers in social sciences may be similar but will never be the same. This is because each of us is different at a micro level. Max Weber (a great researcher, who's contributions we will be reading in the next chapter) would have called this similarity of meaning of different individuals as a 'proximate' or average meaning, signifying that the meaning in the context of the plurality of actors can be similar but not the same.

During my brief career as a qualitative researcher, I have seen many researchers discounting these individual differences and only eyeing larger patterns for the broader community/sample studied. While finding patterns of similarities can be helpful, a qualitative researcher should also attempt to see the differences at an individual level, not just from the perspective of finding outliers but also to understand what makes an individual who they are at a personal level.

Cultural Meaning is when a collective of individuals have similar meanings or thoughts about certain things. It is to be noted that cultural meaning cannot exist without a collective of individuals coming together to attach similar meanings to certain things. Only the subjective meaning of an individual, which is not shared by another group of individuals or a community, may not be considered as a cultural meaning. There might be differences at a micro level even within the larger shared cultural meaning of people. These differences are often known as sub-cultures. Further, there might be a collective of individuals who may not agree with the meaning attached to certain things by the larger (majority/normative part) of the society – commonly known as the counterculture.

Understanding the meaning of words: Every year, while teaching qualitative research to postgraduate students, I conduct an exercise to explain to them how even the meaning of simple and everyday words are different for each of us, but there is also some similarity. I show the students a list of words and ask them to pick just one and then define the word they have chosen (and they are not allowed to look up the definition on their phones).

Some of these words I used for this exercise are as follows.

Love, Joy, Ecstatic, Success, Gravity, Sun, Chemical X, Google, Bark, Epistemology, Simoom

Most students would not choose words such as simoom and epistemology. This is because they would not be aware of the words or may not be sure of their meanings. Even I was not aware of the word 'simoom' until I found it in the dictionary for this exercise. Rarely, I would come across students who would have heard or read about the word 'epistemology' (as most students in India's premium management institutes are from an engineering background). Due to the lack of awareness of these difficult words such as simoom and epistemology, most students would choose the easier words such as love, joy, or success for the exercise. There has been only once when a student had chosen 'epistemology' and defined it (that student actually ended up defining ontology instead) and clearly wanted to impress the class and me! Unfortunately, to me, the student came across as 'wannabe' and a 'show off'. (Although I mostly attempt to create a safe space in the class, I sometimes judge my students – I am human too!). I was quick to perceive that the student was trying to show off because I, too, was a wannabe nerd. (Refer to the '1-word challenge a day' at the end of this book to learn difficult and interesting words such as ontology and epistemology, often used in the philosophy of research).

Once the students would have defined the words of their choice, I would ask them to form groups based on the words selected. So, all the students who chose to define 'love' would be in one group, others who chose 'joy' would be in another group, and so on. Then, I would ask each of these groups to read their definitions to their group members and note the similarities and differences. Once all the students shared their subjective meanings in their respective groups, I would then ask them to come up with a revised definition that they felt represented the word better. The students were allowed to either craft a new definition that included parts of definitions from all the students, or choose a definition written by a single student if they felt that it did justice to the word. Most of the time, the students would mix and match the definitions that the group had discussed to come up with a new one. This exercise would often tell me about the students who had more influence over the group than others. This is because the student with higher influencing power would have most of their subjective definition included in the new definition chosen and agreed upon by the group, i.e., the cultural definition. At times, students whose subjective definitions would be dropped entirely were the ones who found it difficult to mingle with the group or could not put forth their definitions in a manner that they be heard and accepted.

So what did the students learn from this exercise?

- We use several words on a daily basis to communicate and express ourselves, assuming that what these words mean for us is also what they mean to other individuals/groups who are at the receiving end of the communication. The meanings for most words used in daily discourse are different for every individual. What is similar is the broad idea/sentiment around the words.

- The delta (or difference between) our definition of a word compared to the definition of another individual is much higher for emotionally-loaded words such as 'love', 'joy', 'ecstatic' as compared to proper nouns (names of people, organisation, or place; for instance, Google), or words defined in the context of science (e.g. gravity). Now, let us understand this with a stereotypical example. If two scientists meet to define a word such as the planet 'Sun' in comparison to two poets meeting to define the same, the chances of the scientists' definitions being similar to each other is higher than the poets'. This is because the poets' definitions and meanings attached to this word can be more emotional or romantic than the scientists'! But hey, I am not saying that the definition of a scientist is better than that of a poet. Which definition is better would depend on the context. For instance, if a scientist defines the planet 'Sun' in the words of a poet in an academic paper, the chances of the paper being rejected during peer review are quite high. As qualitative researchers, instead of worrying about finding a better definition, we should strive to understand different perspectives, emotions, and the contexts in which these words are used. The context and emotion of a friend telling you to 'fuck off' while playing a video game will be different from that of a stranger telling you to 'fuck off' in a parking lot. Also, take the physical setting/environment into consideration for interpreting the meaning of the word in a better way.

- We try to stay away from the words that we do not know, are not sure of, or words that have two meanings (a homonym; for example, bark). At times, when we use words that are not used in everyday discourse, we want to exhibit our intelligence or higher vocabulary. When I had joined the PhD programme, I was learning about new big academic words and phrases every day. Initially, I would use these words in non-academic spaces with friends and family in everyday conversations to project myself as a cool and learned person (told you – I, too, was a wannabe). I knew that they may not be aware of or exposed to such academic jargon but still used them to stroke my ego. Over the years, I have learnt that a good qualitative researcher would use words to communicate effectively and not announce to the world that they are truly intellectual. Knowing these academic words will help you in the academic discourse, but try not to be an academic asshole (implies both in academic and non-academic spaces). Imagine going to the field to conduct qualitative research and speaking in an academic tone to people/participants who would not understand it. It will do you no good. Not only will you be misunderstood, but you will also not be able to build a rapport and get rich data.

- Few organisations, brands, and individuals 'own' some words. Students who had chosen the word 'Chemical X' had watched or been fans of 'The Powerpuff Girls'. You can do a Google search and see for yourself – the most associated term with Chemical X is The Powerpuff Girls. Chemical X is not a word used in daily discourse. It was probably coined by the makers of The Powerpuff Girls. Hence, the brand 'The Powerpuff Girls' is strongly associated with the word 'Chemical X'. Can you name a word that is strongly associated with a specific movie or a brand? Think of the movie Harry Potter. Do any words or phrases come to your mind that are primarily associated with the brand Harry Potter? If you have read the

Harry Potter books or watched the movies, I bet there are many examples you can think of. The words from the brand Harry Potter may not be used in everyday discourse. However, brands and companies often use the technique of 'owning' words and phrases. Do you remember which word 'Snickers', the chocolate bar, uses or is associated with? Words such as 'glossy' and 'silky' are commonly used by cosmetics and hair care brands respectively. Similarly, words may be associated with culture and countries. Which words or phrases do you think of when someone tells you 'Japan'? Words/phrases may also be associated with social movements. An example of this could be the word 'queer' or 'intersectionality' often being associated with the feminist movement, or the phrase 'Black Lives Matter' being associated with police brutality and racial violence against black people.

We hear, say, and write several words, phrases and sentences in a day. Often, we take the meaning, context, and history associated with these words for granted. To add to it, we not only take for granted the meanings associated with verbal communication but also the interpretation of non-verbal cues. A wink of an eye, when in the pure form of observation without any interpretations attached to it, is the moment an individual closes one eye while the other eye is open. But, given the context and the environment, when interpreted, a wink could be used to show affection, a non-verbal cue to keep a secret, sexual harassment (depending on the laws of the land), or could be just a reflex to dust particle entering the eye, or even a rare medical disease called the Marcus Gunn syndrome. Given the context, it can have various meanings. I hope you now understand that there is meaning all around us, and it is fascinating to make sense of the world and interpret these meanings as a qualitative researcher.

While conducting research, talking to or interviewing the participants, try to understand what they really mean when they use emotionally loaded words.

For example, when a participant says that they are 'happy', 'fine' or 'not well,' ask them what it really means for them and if they know the reason why they are feeling the way they are feeling.

When a participant says that they have been 'discriminated', first understand what they mean by discrimination and the actions that lead to discrimination. You may also want to see how 'discrimination' may be defined by the law. This will help you understand the gap between instances of discrimination experienced by the participants and the structural support available due to the word's legal definition.

While doing qualitative research for products or services, when the participants say that the product is 'good' or that they 'did not like it so much', ask them what they mean when they say the same. What makes the product/service good or bad?

Remember to be curious, just like a child, and ask

> **questions even when they seem obvious and naïve. You may not just surprise yourself but also discover richer data for analysis! But do not ask to define the meaning of each word that the participants say as you may end up irritating them. Keep the conversation natural and smooth.**

Sometimes, at the end of the course, few students tell me that though they now understand qualitative research theoretically, they need to do more practice to be good at it. I always tell them that the world is their 'field'. You can start practising qualitative research by observing yourself, the people in your living room, the people that you might be interacting with within the square boxes of a Zoom call, at public spaces such as train stations, or the airport. Start understanding and questioning the current meaning attached to things by you and the reasons they are different or similar to other people's meanings. Do not wait for this chapter or the book to get over before you conduct qualitative research!

Now, before building our theoretical base more substantial, let us do an exercise.

> **Exercise 1.3: A kickass campaign by Always!**
>
> Always, an American company manufacturing menstrual hygiene products, came up with a campaign/advertisement called '#LikeAGirl' in 2014. The advertisement asked individuals from different age groups (including young school-going girls and boys)

what the phrase like a girl' meant to them.

What does it mean in your culture when someone says 'like a girl'? Does it have any abstract meaning attached to it at a cultural level? Is there any difference between the literal meaning of the phrase and your subjective or cultural meaning?

To watch the advertisement, search 'Always Like a Girl Advertisement' on YouTube.

(Reference: Video Title: Always #LikeAGirl; Channel Name: Always; Link: https://www.youtube.com/watch?v=XjJQBjWYDTs; Accessed on 20th February, 2021)

Can you think of any such phrase or word that has a deeper abstract or a different cultural meaning attached to it when compared to its literal meaning?

Take some time and list down 5 such examples in the space given below. You can use the internet to find such examples for this exercise.

The headwater of meaning (Hermeneutics): I am writing this book thinking that I will be able to explain the concepts of qualitative research to you. But when you read it, you may attach a different meaning to the text. (I hope maybe to not everything you are reading because that would mean I am a terrible writer.) Even when I can effectively communicate to you the concepts in this book to an extent, - you will have somewhat similar ideas and reflections of various qualitative research concepts, but it will not be exactly the same when compared to mine or any other qualitative researcher. Further, since the time of me writing anything in this book and you reading the book, it is likely that you will lose some of the meanings/concepts that I wanted to explain to you, as you may not read it the way I would have thought you will read this book. Funny thing is that I may not be able to write exactly what I feel about qualitative research due to my inability to express my feelings accurately in words. Even when I am trying to express myself through words, there is a loss of meaning when I attempt to find the right words. Since evolution, our language and vocabulary have increased immensely, but, can we really express exactly how we feel? Have you ever observed that you feel something but cannot put it in words or even when you do put it in words, they do not do justice to the feelings? This is because we start losing the meaning of things as we try to put them in words and express them through our relatively developed yet limited language and vocabulary. Hence, when I try and put my thoughts and feelings about qualitative research on paper, there is a loss of meaning in transition. When you read this book, you might have your interpretations of what is given in the book and the way you understand it (adding to further loss of meaning). Further, your understanding may be different or similar but not the same from other readers' understanding and from the understanding that I have of the subject. Hence, we encounter a loss of meaning at every stage of the process. **Does this remind you of a game called Chinese Whispers?**

Let us take religious books as an example and how they may be interpreted differently by different groups of people while often claiming that their meaning attached to the text is the 'real' meaning and better than the other groups. What is written in a religious book may be interpreted differently by different readers. Hence, within some religions, you may have different schools of thought as the meaning attached to religious teachings or books is different for people/groups. In fact, hermeneutics, as a technique, was first used to interpret the Bible and to capture the 'true' message that the Bible gives to the people and to avoid multiple interpretations by different individuals. For the time being, you need to understand that hermeneutics is a method of interpretation used to understand the intended and subjective meaning associated mostly with text and verbal communications, and if possible, even with non-verbal communication.

There are also times when we intentionally do not want to express the things that we really think or feel. It could be due to various reasons such as an individual being introverted, not able to trust the person with whom they are going to share the information, or the individual may be guided by the **language of everyday morality**. What is the language of everyday morality? We all have come across people who we do not like (or hate from our guts). Common examples of this could be your boss or your sneaky ass-licking colleague who would do unnecessary politics to get ahead of you, or your classmate, or an individual who would want to look smarter or gain pleasure at your cost! We all have come across such people and have been in some toxic relationships. However, often, we are not able to say or express what we really think about these people due to a sense of morality guiding our communication. For instance, there have been times when I wanted to tell my ex-colleague that he is stupid, but can I say this to him on his face? You bet not.

Question: When was the last time you felt something but were either not able to express it or expressed yourself differently from how you really felt?

Exercise 1.4: I did/didn't mean that!

Linda Sarsour, an American activist, in a 2017 speech, expressed the need to defend and protect Muslims against the Trump administration (the same year Trump introduced a travel ban, also infamously known as the 'Muslim ban'). Linda was criticised for her speech on national news channels and media. Here is a short excerpt from her speech. Can you guess the reason for her criticism?

"...I hope that when we stand up to those who oppress our communities, that Allah accepts from us that as a form of jihad, that we are struggling against tyrants and rulers not only abroad in the Middle East or the other side of the world, but here in the

United States of America, where you have fascists and white supremacists and Islamophobes reigning in the White House..."

Any guesses why Linda was criticised?

She was called out because she used the word *'jihad'* to criticise the Trump administration. What is your understanding of the word *'jihad'* and can you recall what influenced your understanding of this word?

Jihad, as a word, has various interpretations. However, the interpretation that *jihad* is associated with the most, especially by the majority of non-Muslim individuals in Western society, is that of the act of terrorism. Clearly, the meaning attributed to the word *jihad* by Linda was different from the proximate meaning given by the majority of the society. The association of terrorism with the word is primarily because the mainstream western media has reinforced the meaning by using the word *'jihad'* mainly in the context of terrorism (for the majority of their society).

Here, the larger cultural meaning and sentiment (in the United States) with the word *'jihad'* is considered negative, and individuals such as Linda Sarsour want to change this narrative. I feel that Linda used the word in her speech knowing that she might face backlash. This was her way of showing – to the larger society – how minority and marginalised communities are forced to assimilate with the larger normative society.

Feminists have often used this technique to use words that are generally avoided in the larger discourse by using them in everyday conversation, thus making the word lose the meaning that it had previously. One such word is 'queer', which was primarily used as an insult but is now not just used by queer individuals to reclaim identities but also in the popular discourse as a cool way of pointing to something different!

Let us begin the exercise. In the space given below, write down:

    a)   Instances where you tried to communicate something, but it was taken as something else by the individual/group at the receiving end of the conversation. What did you do once you realised that your message was not interpreted the way you wanted or thought that it would be?

b) Instances where you have purposely used words that are somewhat taboo in everyday discourse due to morality governing everyday language and behaviour?

c) An instance where there was a misinterpretation of meaning primarily due to the difference in identities and cultures of individuals/groups involved in the communication?

What makes an interpretation awesome and scientific?

Remember, your interpretations should be based on or grounded in observations or other forms of data. Let me make a generalisation. We, human beings, have a habit of jumping to conclusions quickly. Having great interpretations does not mean giving meaning to things immediately. On the contrary, it means staying with just the observation for some time and then interpreting it, and, if possible, arriving at interpretations from multiple perspectives.

First, let us understand the difference between observation and interpretation.

Observation is the process of recording and describing the field/data. It is important that when you record and describe data, you do not add your interpretation (meaning) to the same. Let me also tell you that there is a thin line between observation and interpretations (often an overlap), but, as a qualitative researcher, you should ensure that you do not end up over-interpreting. Even though I advise you to keep your observations away from interpretations in the initial stages of practising qualitative research, it will not be entirely possible (it is still not possible for me, even after doing qualitative research for some years now). But, try only recording your observations first and then attach meaning to them. Just having observations will help you to not jump to conclusions and will give you more time for interpretations as compared to how our mind works, where we immediately want to attach meaning to things. This will eventually lead to a better and more well-thought out interpretation of the data.

Few tips/examples of differentiating observations from interpretations:

- Do not say that he or she 'looked happy' while observing, as 'happy' is an interpretation. Describe what they looked like – how their facial expression, body language, tone of voice and actions were. Capture these details before concluding what you thought someone felt like.

- A student, while sharing his observation (after an observation exercise) in the class, said, "I saw a group of *Chinese students* walking in the campus". How did he know that the group of people were Chinese? He had not asked these people about their nationality as he just observed them from a distance. Could they have been from other Asian countries? Definitely! But are individuals with Asian features only citizens of Asian countries? Definitely not! So, without talking to the people, one may want to refrain from assuming where they are from; instead, the student should have noted that their features made him feel that they were from a different culture. Also, how do he know that the group of people were students? That was an interpretation again. What about them made my student feel that the people he was observing were also students? Was it that they looked young, or had college bags or books in their hands which are mostly used by students, or was it their dressing sense, or was it based on the assumption that most people inside the university campus are students? When we make assumptions based on our perceptions, we should be aware that it is our way of understanding reality but may not always be true.

- Suppose, out of nowhere, it has started raining outside (London weather I tell you ;)). I have decided to go outside, being fully aware of bad weather. Now, I have an umbrella, and I have not forgotten about it. In fact, the umbrella is looking right at me, and I am looking right back at it. I still decide to go out without the umbrella, knowing that I will get drenched in the rain. Now, was it a rational choice to not carry the umbrella (what do you all think – was it rational or irrational of me)? I know most of you might be assuming right now that I am barking mad for having an umbrella, not forgetting about it, and still not using it while going out in the rain. But what if I tell you that it was my first London rain and I wanted to dance in it, feel it on my skin – will you still think that the decision was irrational? (Some of you must be still judging me for my desire to dance in water that has microplastic pollution!) And what if I told you that I looked at the umbrella, but I knew that it was broken and of no use, thus deciding to go outside without it (obviously to get some work done for which I could have not waited till the rain stops)? Will you still think that I was irrational?

So, what is rational or irrational behaviour also depends on the context, – of actions that give maximum satisfaction given the prior information and knowledge than an individual has. You may think of an individual's behaviour as irrational without knowing their context and reasons behind those behaviours.

I want to emphasise that in the initial phase of doing qualitative research, try to just record observations, and try harder not to attach meaning immediately, leading to direct interpretations. Further, try to have thick observations – that is, record as much as you can in the form of writing and drawing.

Now let us do a quick observation exercise.

Exercise 1.5: I was only observing

Get dressed to go out. Carry a small writing pad or few sheets of paper and a pen or two along with it (this is the primary gear of qualitative researchers – a qualitative researcher without a pen and paper is like a wizard without its wand!)

Find a spot and be comfortable. Ensure that you choose a safe spot – do not stand in the middle of the road or the edge of a building to make observations. Ensure that you have access to the space you are going to (for instance, at a railway station, please buy a platform ticket). If going to a crowded public space, try carrying a mask and a hand sanitiser.

Do this observation exercise for at least an hour. Remember to write as much as you can to record your observations. Your brain will not remember everything you observe – stop being lazy and write.

In case, for some reason, you cannot venture out of your house, do the observation from the window/door of your house.

~

Reflect on the questions below once you have completed the observation exercise of 60 minutes

It might take you another 30 minutes to reflect on these questions.

Here are a few questions that you can reflect on:

How was the entire process of observation for you? Why?

Were you able to respect time, i.e., could you observe for at least an hour? Did you finish early or did you end up spending more than an hour or precisely for an hour on the exercise?

I ask you this question because, initially, I have seen many of my students struggle to observe for an hour. If you have struggled too, you will need to do more observation exercises. If you did more than an hour, congratulations – you have already started enjoying qualitative research (I can see your dedication). If you finish precisely in one hour,   you are someone who takes instructions seriously – I like the respect you have given me and to this exercise :)

How was the note-taking process for you? Were you able to 'thick' the description? Why?

Did you use your senses other than sight such as hearing, smell, touch, or maybe even taste?

Most of the time, I have seen my students only writing about what they see (or data captured only visually) and they tend to ignore the data captured through other senses. It might not be possible to capture data through all the senses during observations – for instance, you may not have any data for 'taste', but you will likely have data related to hearing, smell or even touch when you touched the objects that you interacted with. If you have not recorded these data points, take this as a learning and remember it the next time you are doing observations.

In case you went out to observe, did other people notice you? Did you want to show people that you are a cool researcher and flaunted your diary and pen – taking notes in a way that people would be sure to notice you?

Let me tell you an interesting story behind why I have asked you this question. I was once conducting a qualitative research session in Delhi with executive master's students (all working in the industry and studying a part-time MBA programme). I asked all the students to observe outside the campus but somewhere near as they had to return with their observations within an hour. Close to the class, there was a temple, outside which, there were beggars, flower peddlers, and illegal hawkers selling *prasad* to be offered by devotees to the Gods (a usual sight in India). Now, four of my students chose to conduct their observation outside the temple. On seeing these students, all the vendors, peddlers, hawkers, and beggars ran away. They thought that the students were officers from the government taking stock of things outside the temple. This created havoc in the existing ecosystem. Although this gave us a perspective on power distance between the people at the bottom of the pyramid and the bureaucracy, this was not the observation's objective. We will be discussing ethics in research, types of observations (participatory and non-participatory), and covert and overt research in the next few chapters in detail. But what I want you to understand is that even when a researcher goes to collect data as an outsider (i.e. thought to be someone different by the community), the researcher strives to become one with the community, to build a rapport, and to share common grounds. Most of the time, the researcher should not want to make themselves 'the other' on purpose to the community or individuals that they are interacting with and collecting data from. For shorter and non-participatory observations, building a rapport may not be possible or be the objective. However, as a qualitative researcher, you must know that when people are aware that they are being observed, their behaviour might change. Do not scare or raise suspicion of your participants or the community where you are conducting research!

Do not worry if you were not satisfied with the way you observed – most of us struggle with it initially and, as they say, every champion was a noob once! Remember to take baby steps. Welcome to the world of qualitative research :)

Once you have finished your observation and reflected on the questions above, go back to your observation and check if there have been places where you have made assumptions, added meaning, or done interpretations.

What happens once observations are complete?

Once you have made the observations, you will take some time to interpret the data, which will be done through the process of coding (do not worry, you do not have to do coding/data analysis for the above exercise; we have it covered in the latter part of this book!). The objective of doing this is to help you to come up with a better interpretation that is grounded in data. Following this process will enable you to have rational explanations of your interpretation. In simple terms, it is like providing reasoning for your interpretations.

So, remember these three broad steps:

Observations (here you just describe the data that your senses capture) → Interpretation (here you try to give meaning to what you have observed by analysing the data from observation, ensuring that you are true to the data) → Explanation (where you explain why you have interpreted what you have interpreted). There may be multiple interpretations and explanations. Try to capture as much as you can. It is not necessary that you have to do observation, interpretation, and explanation in different stages. However, segregating them initially has helped me a lot, and I hope it helps you. Once you get used to doing more observations, the overlap between these stages will increase. But try not to jump the gun with immediate interpretations and explanations in the initial stages!

See you in the next chapter!

CHAPTER 2
HISTORY AND EVOLUTION OF QUALITATIVE RESEARCH

Whenever I teach qualitative research, I ensure that I cover the history of qualitative research in the initial classes. Often before starting the class, the students ask me questions such as:

But why do we need to know about history?

How is it going to help us?

Can't we get our hands dirty doing research, instead of studying about the past?

The ability to do qualitative research will be one of the most essential skills that any individual should have in the coming times. To understand why, we need to know a little about qualitative research's evolution and history.

Historically (and, sometimes, even today), qualitative research has often not been considered rigorous and relevant. Few academicians still think and teach their students (ignoring the research objective) that quantitative methods are the only way to go about. At times, qualitative researchers are ridiculed and told that they are not researchers, but storytellers. As a qualitative researcher, I, too, have heard such comments. Some schools in social sciences such as anthropology, sociology, gender studies, and psychology are more accepting of qualitative research than other schools such as management studies (even though the qualitative case study method is now widely used in management studies). If you are a research professional working in the industry, you may have to sensitise your colleagues and even superiors about the merit of qualitative research for accomplishing various business objectives. This is primarily because many in the industry have little to no idea about qualitative research methods and their applicability in the business context.

But, ever wondered why even those trained as quantitative researchers ridicule qualitative research methods and qualitative researchers? Well, there are many reasons, but the gist of it is that they are scared of everything qualitative! They are scared of understanding and conducting qualitative research because of its fluidity, primarily because their minds have been trained to think in the binary. They are scared that if they attempt qualitative research, they would not be able to capture the complexities, would not be able to have thick descriptions, and meaningfully interpret the data. The debate of qualitative research versus quantitative research has been going on since the 19th century!

A good researcher will always chart the research methodology after understanding the research objectives and questions. You may decide to become a qualitative researcher, but you need to understand that not all research questions and objectives will fall under the purview of qualitative research (or under quantitative research). As researchers, we need to understand the strengths and limitations of any research methodology. Hence, even when you may want to specialise in qualitative, quantitative, or mixed-method research, you will need to have basic knowledge of all the methodologies and understand their nature and applicability. Only then you can select or suggest a methodology most suitable given the research objectives and questions.

A brief understanding of the history and evolution of qualitative research would build our foundation to understand:

What is qualitative research?

Why do we need qualitative research?

When should qualitative research methods be used?

How is it different from quantitative research?

Don't worry, this chapter does not aim to make you a historian on research methods, neither will I throw at you many names, citations, and references that confuse you further. Take the text below as a conversation with a friend – a conversation you are having just before writing an exam for which you have not studied well, and your friend is attempting to summarise the concepts.

Personally, I do not think that there is a 'father/mother' or one specific individual who started qualitative research. This is because qualitative research is interdisciplinary and is built on thoughts, theories, methods, and tools contributed by various schools and faculties of social sciences (at times, even using natural sciences to strengthen its case for the need to have a different methodology for understanding society and human behaviour). A simple Google search might throw up some names as the founding father or the daddy of qualitative research – do not fall into that trap! Now, I am not discounting these names for what they have offered to the field of qualitative research, just that I do not think that there is one particular person who could be said to have begun it all.

Let us begin by understanding the manner in which we gain knowledge, that is, the philosophical paradigms in research. These can be classified into the broad categories of 'positivism' and 'interpretivism'. Positivism and interpretivism are to be viewed on a linear scale with one at each end (and not in the form of a binary). This means that we can also gain knowledge by mixing and matching methods and tools from both positivist and interpretivist paradigms. Further, it also implies that some methods and tools could be considered more positivist or radical, while others could be more on the interpretivist side in the spectrum. This certainly does not mean that a method and tool on the spectrum's extreme ends are better than those in the middle. What is good would depend on the questions, objectives, and limitations that the researcher has while doing the research.

To simplify it further, let us understand this with the help of the political spectrum. If we were to represent political thoughts on a linear scale, on the extreme right, we would have the far-right, and on the extreme left, we would have the radical left. At the centre of this linear scale, we would have something/someone called the centre or moderate. Further, between the centre and the far left, we would have the liberals. Similarly, between the far-right and centre, we would have the conservatives. There would be instances where you will also see an overlap between the schools of thought; for instance, an individual might identify as a liberal but may be conservative when it comes to LGBTQ rights. Or an individual may be conservative but support healthcare for all (or, at least, for most, if not all). However, unlike the political spectrum, research philosophy is based on scientific methods (although there are debates on which methods are more scientific, thus leading to the positivism versus interpretivism discourse), but I hope you get the envisioning of linear representation of philosophising how we gain knowledge.

But what is positivism?

The term positivism was coined by Auguste Comte (in the 19th century). Positivism, as a paradigm of the philosophy of research, is based on the foundation that knowledge should be objective – one that is free from human subjectivity (and not impacted by our belief systems and biases). There are other characteristics of positivism, but for us (and, for the time being), the important thing to understand is that it emphasises doing research free from the influence of human values and subjectivity.

But how did positivism foray into the social sciences?

Once upon a time, (during the 18th and 19th century), while social science, as a field, was emerging, few social scientists suggested and propagated that social sciences research could follow the footsteps of natural/pure sciences (that include subjects such as Physics, Mathematics, Chemistry, etc.).

They discussed among themselves:

"We might not be as cool as the natural and pure scientists, but we are smart. We can do what they have been doing," said Social Scientist 1.

"What do you mean, how can you do that?" asked Social Scientist 2.

"All we need to do is be inspired by their methods and techniques and use them to understand people and society," said Social Scientist1.

"I still don't get it. Should we not come up with our way of doing research and seeking knowledge?" Social Scientist 2 who seemed concerned.

"Just shut the fizz up! It's better than not doing anything and only thinking about new methods to gain knowledge in social sciences. Besides, it's much easier to copy. I mean, to be inspired, and I don't want to die poor." said Social Scientist 3 looking at Social Scientists 2 and 1 in desperation.

"I have got this. See, just like in math, if any individual adds two and two, the answer will always be four — it does not matter if the individual is from Berlin or London or New York, what age and gender they are, what religion they identify with, or the political ideology they belong to, the answer will always be four (given that the individual knows addition). So, we can use similar techniques and methodology in social sciences that enables the researcher to be completely objective; thus, anyone doing research will always get the same findings irrespective of what they believe in or where they are from," beamed Social Scientist 1.

"Yes, just like the law of gravity! It does not matter if you are a living or a non-living being, if you are a good person or a bad person – if you fall from the Eiffel Tower, you are coming straight down," noted Social Scientist 2.

"Ahh! I get it now. Let's do it. Let's bring this thought and way of doing research in social sciences!" said Social Scientist 3.

Caution: The above dialogue is fictional. Take it with a pinch of salt. No offence was given. Although it is true that many social scientists, even some of the comparatively famous ones, were (and still are) poor or at the mercy of the university contracts!

The gist is that more and more social scientists in the late 18th and 19th century started adopting methods and tools often used in pure/natural sciences. Their expectations and processes (to understand society) were similar to that of natural/pure science – stressing objectivity, free from human bias, and having generalisable results or results that were 'true' for the larger population. Also, the important bit – quantitative researchers are from the positivist school of thought. At times, positivist approaches and quantitative research are used interchangeably.

During the 19th century, the positivist way of doing social sciences research was widely gaining popularity. Further, researchers and social scientists were adding to the knowledge of doing positivist research in social sciences. One such researcher was Charles Booth (known for 17 volumes of the *Life and Labour of the People in London*). Within the positivist paradigm and the field of sociology, he was known to have classified poverty in a way that captured its real/true extent among the labour class.

For example, a country decides that anyone earning less than five dollars a day would fall under the poverty line. Seems quite simple to identify who is poor then, right? Just take the population's survey or existing government records, and you will know what percentage of people earn less than 5 dollars a day – they would account for 'poor people' in the country. Also, as per this logic, people who earn the least will be considered the poorest. Let us demonstrate this:

Individual 1: A farmer, who barely earns anything (definitely earns less than 5 dollars a day) but can feed himself from the crop that he grows.

Individual 2: A single mother of two, who earns less than 5 dollars a day and has two children dependent on her.

Individual 3: A criminal whose daily earning from pick-pocketing is not known.

Individual 4: An immigrant who earns less than 5 dollars a

day.

Individual 5: An individual who earns than 10 dollars a day but is homeless.

Here are a few questions for you:

Can you say that poverty impacts all of these individuals in the same way?

Do you think having one uniform social policy to address poverty will help the country address real problems?

According to Charles Booth, poverty is relative, and a standard definition to determine who is poor just with one criteria/variable (that of income) as the measurement parameter was not sufficient. His work popularised the use of multiple variables to make sense of quantitative data and introduced a relatively more humanistic way of conducting quantitative research. Apart from surveys (as a quantitative research tool), Booth was also known to record his observations, subjective experiences, and feelings while understanding poverty in the labour class. Knowingly or unknowingly, he contributed a lot to the foundation of the interpretative paradigm. This also led other researchers to think about frameworks that could be adopted to understand human behaviour and society.

Thus, several researchers and social scientists started rethinking how research could be conducted, and knowledge can be gained in social sciences. This not just led to the development in the overall positivist framework and quantitative research methodology but also led to the birth of a new framework called 'interpretivism'. As in the earlier days, interpretivism's reference point was positivism, and foundations were based on the critiques of the positivist school of thought – it was also known as anti-positivism, anti-naturalism and by various other names by positivist researchers. In simple words, interpretivism was treated as a framework that was opposite to positivism. Interpretivists took this name-calling to heart and started terming positivist research as non-interpretivism. And so, ever since then – since the time these thoughts/frameworks were taking shape – the us versus them tussle has existed. But, on the brighter side, these debates make any kind of science (social or pure/natural science) cool – as it is only through questioning that we gain knowledge.

Do not worry about the different names of interpretivism and positivism that you come across while reading different books. Also, very likely, you will only encounter these names in academics (especially the schools of philosophy and sociology). If you are a practitioner, then all you need to know is the following:

- That quantitative research method mainly falls under the positivist framework. Similarly, qualitative research falls under the interpretive framework.
- That the primary philosophies governing positivism (quantitative research) and interpretivism (qualitative research will help you understand the advantages and limitations of using these frameworks.

So, what were some of the significant criticisms of positivism that led to the development of the interpretative framework?

The Chicago School (a group of sexy sociologists and researchers) is known for developing alternate frameworks/methods of doing research in social sciences. But even before that, sociologists and researchers such as Max Weber had criticised and expressed the positivist framework's limitations. One of the most significant critiques was that while understanding society and human behaviour, it was difficult for researchers to be free from their subjective meanings and biases (irrespective of the framework used). Subjectivity is what makes individuals (human beings) unique. Further, every knowledge of society is based on this subjective understanding of its individuals (we studied about subjective meaning in Chapter 1). We are not even aware and conscious of all our biases and subjective understandings of the world, so, how can we be free from them? Even when we observe something new – something that we have not observed before – we attach meaning to it based on our past experiences. Further, in the positivist framework, even the understanding of cause and effect (causal mechanisms), is not free from the subjective meaning attached by the researcher. If you ask me, in social sciences research, an individual/researcher cannot completely be objective, and if they claim to be so, then they are not human!

Food for thought: On the one hand, interpretive framework or qualitative researchers criticise positivism and quantitative research in social sciences for not being free from subjectivity while they themselves are not objective. Is this hypocrisy?

Well, interpretivism is not free from subjectivity; in fact, it celebrates it. It is based on the foundation that we attach subjective meaning to the world, and that subjectivity is not a bad thing. We can try and be aware/mindful of subjective meanings (though we will not be aware of all of them as we are blind to many of our subjectivities and biases). But, as researchers, when we are aware of our subjectivities, we should state them and try to understand why and how we attach these meanings. As qualitative researchers, we should also celebrate the subjective meaning given by the people and communities that we are studying. Only when we acknowledge and see value in these subjective meanings, will we truly understand what leads people to attach these meanings – the reasons for having these meanings may be rational or irrational.

Another school of thought within qualitative research on dealing with subjectivity is where the researcher indulges in 'bracketing' (used especially by some phenomenologists – phenomenology is a form of qualitative research method that we will read about in this book later). For now, we need to understand that bracketing is the process where the researcher tries to set aside their experiences, so the research finding or the knowledge is not influenced by their subjectivity.

Irrespective of what you decide to do as a qualitative researcher – either acknowledge that you cannot get rid of these subjective meanings or try to bracket them as much as possible to have findings/exploration that is free from your subjectivity – always remember to acknowledge these subjectivities, values, beliefs systems, worldviews, and biases. Also, acknowledge and let your readers know how you have dealt with these subjectivities. Acknowledging these aspects is the most important thing before you pick a school of thought.

If you ask me how I treat subjectivity, I would say that initially, I thought that I was from the first school of thought, which believes that one can never bracket themselves completely or be free from their subjective experiences and interpretations. But, over time, while doing research, I have learnt a lot about myself. As a qualitative researcher, irrespective of it being planned or unplanned, you will learn a lot about who you are as a person. This process of learning will be continuous. Every interaction, observation, and interpretation you arrive at also tells something about you as a researcher (you will notice some of them and know yourself better, or even feel that this was not you, but it was!). I have realised some of my biases impact how I do research and perhaps even its outcome. Hence, I attempt to be aware of these critical biases and bracket them to be a better researcher. I would say that I identify with both the schools of thought on treating subjectivity within qualitative research, though mostly I relate to the first school and believe that it is not possible to bracket the self from the self!

If you are working in the industry, most of the times, your clients may not be interested in knowing your subjectivities and will focus on the 'research findings' that help their strategic decision-making process and, ultimately, the business. Even when you don't share your subjectivities and how you have treated them, be aware of them and acknowledge them. There will be times when doing this will help you present your findings in a better fashion, and you will grow as a researcher.

I hope you are now aware of some fundamental differences between positivism and interpretivism (as well as quantitative and qualitative research).

Cool! So, this discourse/debate on how research within social sciences is to be conducted has raged for quite some time now. However, interpretivism (qualitative research) started picking up when companies (from capitalist societies) started understanding and using it to make more profits. It was and is still used for marketing, advertising, and selling products and services to the customers. However, compared to quantitative research or the positivist approach, qualitative research is still not as popular. The truth for many cultures/societies is that they put research and knowledge in natural, pure sciences, and STEM education before the knowledge in social sciences, humanities, and arts, and it is because of this orphan behaviour towards the social sciences and related fields that researchers within social science still attempt to copy (or get inspired from) research methods from natural/pure sciences even when it is not required. It is a way to tell the society that social scientists are no less than pure/natural scientists (remember the conversation between three researchers? ;))

Exercise 2.1. Can you answer the following questions?

First, try answering these questions on your own. Once you have done that, read up online, search different academic papers, websites or revisit this chapter to see if you have understood these concepts. Trust me, when you search for knowledge from multiple sources, you learn more.

What is positivism?

What is interpretivism?

What are some of the critiques of a positivist framework?

(Now, you shall be subjected to questions whose answers are not mentioned directly in this chapter,

but if you think about what you have learnt, answering them would not be difficult)

Can you think of some advantages of using a positivist framework or quantitative research?

Can you think of some limitations of interpretive framework or qualitative research?

Reading recommendation: I would highly recommend you to read the book 'Gang Leader for a Day: A Rogue

Sociologist Takes to the Streets' by Sudhir Venkatesh, which has helped me understand qualitative research better, and to realise that our expected experiences of the field/process of the research can be different from the actual experience. I think I read the book at the right time – during the initial years of my research journey. Through Sudhir's journey, I understood that we all start as naïve researchers and that the field teaches us things that are not necessarily taught in the classrooms. I also learned that as a social sciences researcher, irrespective of what and how much I know, I should always remain naïve – as it grounds me to continue learning, helps in knowing my limitations, and enables me to acknowledge that I can capture or only attempt to capture only a small part of fragmented and multiple realities.

The book is easy to read, flows smoothly, and pushes you to spend some time reflecting. I often questioned myself while reading the book: "What would I do in a situation that Sudhir was in?" Pick up the book and ask yourself such questions while reading – trust me, you will not regret it!

Reference:

Venkatesh, S.A. (2008). Gang leader for a day: A rogue sociologist takes to the streets. Penguin Press.

CHAPTER 3
WHAT IS QUALITATIVE RESEARCH?

We are in the third chapter of this book, but do we understand what qualitative research really is?

I feel it is difficult to define. The beauty of qualitative research is that it borrows theories, methods, and tools from various schools of social sciences such as sociology, anthropology, and psychology.

If I have to draw a comparison, then it is similar to management studies. You will find various definitions of what management is, but actually, management studies take its theories, paradigms, methods, and tools from various schools of social sciences as well as pure sciences. An individual exposed to management studies or pursuing their bachelor's/master's degree in Business Studies (MBA and similar degree) knows that they are studying theories from various fields of social sciences. Further, they also study the application of pure sciences subjects such as mathematics, and operations management in meeting business goals. Although qualitative research does not borrow theories from pure sciences directly, its foundation is based on various subjects/schools of social sciences.

During my live sessions, students get disappointed when I say that it is difficult to define qualitative research. It is unacceptable to our minds to not have definitions (to not attach meaning: remember Chapter 1) for a subject that we are studying or are invested in. So, here is a definition – especially for those who cannot do without one:

"Qualitative research is multimethod in focus, involving an interpretative, naturalistic approach to its subject matter. This means that qualitative researchers study things in their natural settings, attempting to make sense of, or interpret, phenomena in terms of the meanings people bring to them. Qualitative research involves the studied use and collection of a variety of empirical materials – case study, personal experience, introspective, life story, interview, observational, historical, interactional, and visual texts – that describe routine and problematic moments and meanings in individuals' lives." (Denzin and Lincoln 2005:2; taken from Aspers, P & Corte, U; 2019)

However, Aspers & Corte have criticised this definition of qualitative research for being more on what qualitative research comprises rather than what it is. A rising trend that I have witnessed these days is that qualitative research is being used in settings that may not be considered 'natural environments'. Nowadays 'qualitative experiments' are being conducted where individuals/groups are tested in an environment specifically created for the research.

Characteristics of qualitative research:

This list describing the characteristics of qualitative research is not exhaustive. I have tried to present to you some primary characteristics of qualitative research. Reflecting on these characteristics would not just help you understand what qualitative research is but also how it should be conducted or envisioned.

- Aims for an in-depth understanding: Qualitative research aims to get at the bottom of the iceberg. It aims to understand the 'why' of the meaning that we give to this world. And we have seen in Chapter 1 that there are different types of meanings (e.g. subjective meaning, cultural meaning). An excellent qualitative study would also aim to understand the 'why's of why'. It is something like the '5 Why' concept used to determine the root cause/problems used in operations management ('5 Why' in the context of operations management is a technique where the individual often keeps asking 'why' to eventually identify the deeper problem – it is believed that most of the time, one can reach the root cause by asking 'why' five times, hence, the name '5 Why'). Now, I am not suggesting that a qualitative researcher needs to ask 'why' five times to make sense of the deeper meaning. Instead, a qualitative researcher needs to be curious to understand the deeper meanings behind actions, behaviours, symbols, phenomena, social and material circumstances – broadly in the community/environment/society that (as researchers) we may be immersed in.

- Fragmented and multiple realities: As qualitative researchers, we need to understand that we are capturing only a small fragment of the reality (even when we strive to capture the reality as is). Further, realities are multiple in social sciences unlike in pure or natural sciences, and we may be able to capture only a few perspectives of this multiplicity. This is not just true for qualitative research but also for quantitative research in social sciences. Though the researcher's desire could be to capture complete reality/realities, it is extremely difficult to do so (I do not think it is possible in social sciences). However, our limitations and inabilities to capture the entire reality/realities using scientific methods is not a bad thing - it is just a limitation that needs to be acknowledged. Accepting this enables the researchers (us) to be more rigorous, and motivates us to capture realities through various methods, tools, and frameworks, and allows us to triangulate and validate our interpretations/findings.

- Qualitative research is fluid: Qualitative research adopts a very emergent design. It is perfectly fine to think of using a specific qualitative method or tool while planning the research and adding or using a completely new method or tool while conducting the research. However, the caution here is that wherever such changes occur, the researcher should be able to logically explain why they need to change the method or tools while in the field and how it enables them to capture more meaningful data. As long as the researcher can reason, the methods of data collection can be adaptive for different participants/communities/contexts/settings. The data collected in the researcher's initial phase may also guide the further stages of the research process, hence, making the design emergent.

I have often seen students and even professionals not wanting to change their methods and/or tools even when they realise that they can get richer data through other methods and/or tools. This is largely because they do not want to come across as unsure, or someone who had not planned the study properly, or because of their prior experience in quantitative methods, which is not as fluid as qualitative methods. We should remember that we all learn in the process and that there should be no shame attached to acknowledging that a change in method or tool is required provided we can reason and justify the same.

- Attempts to capture the holistic view of social phenomena while retaining each participant's uniqueness: Though this may vary depending on the objective of your research, generally speaking, a qualitative researcher attempts to capture, connect the dots and give an interconnected reference to the larger phenomenon being studied.

However, few words of caution: I have seen many researchers generalise their research findings to the larger society or, the larger population with qualitative research (often using a very small non-probability sampling, which may not truly represent the population). Remember, that, as a qualitative researcher, in most cases, you would be giving a holistic view of the phenomenon, for the individuals/communities/societies that you have studied. Hence, your findings should be generalised only to the sample/participants you studied and not the larger population/society. Unlike in quantitative research, where there is an emphasis on the sample being representative of the larger population, the sample for qualitative research may not represent the entire community/population. Be cautious when making generalisations, and remember that you are generalising or providing a holistic view only for the people/community/context you have studied. There are some exceptions to this, and these exceptions mostly include a larger sample **size or have a different approach and objective.**

Over the years, I have seen that many researchers just bring out the 'majority voice of the sample' while doing qualitative research and ignore voices from the sample that are different from the majority. To truly understand a phenomenon and capture reality, all distinct voices from different participants should be considered. Let us understand this through a question:

Question: If you interview 10 individuals for a qualitative research project and 8 of them give similar responses, but 2 individuals have very different responses, what will you do? Whose responses/voice will you include or give preference to?

When I ask this question in class, most of my students say that they will include the narrative of 8 individuals who have similar voices and ignore the voices of the 2 individuals as they are different from most others. I see this happening even in the industry, where qualitative researchers only bring out the 'patterns' or the similarities in responses. This is often done because many qualitative researchers think that 8 individuals are 80 percent of the total sample – much larger than the 20 percent (2 individuals). Hence, this 80 percent becomes more critical while presenting the research findings. This approach is not correct – a qualitative researcher should always strive to include all the voices. It is these differences in voices that help qualitative researchers to not oversimplify and enables retaining nuances and complexities. Further, qualitative research is not about saying that 80 percent of the sample think in a certain way and represent the larger population – that is the role of quantitative research with larger sample size. Instead, a qualitative researcher should understand why some participants think, behave or attach a distinct meaning when compared to other participants. And even when these meanings are similar, they will never be the same (remember Chapter 1); further, individuals may have a similar meaning but may conclude to it due to different reasons. As a qualitative researcher, you would want to understand these differences in the voices/perspectives and strive to represent them. Remember, finding patterns and aiming to give a holistic view is essential, but so is retaining the individuality and distinct voices of the participants.

- Celebrating subjectivity: As a qualitative researcher, you will bring in your worldview and interpretations in your research. Know that it is difficult to make a social sciences research completely 'objective'. Though few researchers have suggested different techniques to remain objective while doing qualitative research, can your research be completely free from subjectivity? (I do not think that is possible). Know that you will either capture the participant's perspective of their experience and/or be giving your perspective on the participants' perspectives/behaviours. Subjectivity is not bad, however, you should acknowledge, whenever you can, and be aware of these subjectivities. The funny thing is that by acknowledging your subjectivities in qualitative research, you make the research more 'objective'!

-

Exercise 3.1: How would you define qualitative research?

Let us attempt defining qualitative research. You have read three chapters, and based on whatever you have understood and absorbed so far, what will be your definition of qualitative research? (Remember there is no right definition and no self-judgement). Go ahead, write your definition!

Exercise 3.2: Reflections through 5 Why's

In the next few chapters, we will be reading about qualitative research methods, the most commonly used tools, and how data should be analysed. However, before moving ahead, it is time to reflect.

Take a deep breath, slow down and think about

what is present with you at this point in time? It does not have to be related to qualitative research, it could be about anything from your life. Once you answer the first question below, ask yourself 'why'. We will keep asking ourselves 'why' five times, to see what is really at the root of what we are thinking. Do not worry if you get done before reaching the fifth 'why' or need to ask more than five 'why's.

(Write it down. If you need more space to write, feel free to use a journal/notebook.)

1. What is present with you – right now – at this very moment? Why?

2. Why?

3. Why?

4. Why?

5. Why?

Reference:

Aspers, P., Corte, U. What is Qualitative in Qualitative Research. Qual Sociol 42, 139-160 (2019). Link the reading was accessed on https://link.springer.com/article/10.1007/s11133-019-9413-7. (Accessed date: 8th March, 2021)

CHAPTER 4
QUALITATIVE RESEARCH METHODS

Before starting this chapter, there is an important thing that I would want you to understand:

There is a difference between research methods and research tools used in qualitative research.

I have often seen researchers and industry practitioners confusing some of the research tools as research methods. A research method is an approach you choose while doing qualitative research. In contrast, research tools are the means of collecting data under the research method. Further, multiple research tools may be used under one research method for collecting data. Some research tools work better with specific research methods (in this chapter, we will also understand the reason behind the same). However, let us not overcomplicate things – for now, just remember that there is a fundamental difference between research methods and research tools, and, as qualitative researchers, it is essential to not confuse research tools as methods.

In this chapter, we will be studying the five most commonly used qualitative research methods, when to use them, and their primary research tools. In the next chapter (Chapter 5), we will learn about various research tools in detail. Towards the end of the book, I have also provided a 'cheat sheet' where a summary of all the research methods, tools, and ways of analysing/coding qualitative data is provided for your ready reference. Let us begin!

Section 1 – Narrative Research/Inquiry

When the goal or research objective is to capture voices, opinions, and experiences, we use narrative inquiry. To put it very naïvely – to understand a certain 'narrative' or multiple 'narratives' (recall of experiences, voices, and expressions of emotions related to these experiences shared by individuals, groups and communities), narrative research is used as a qualitative method. Narrative inquiry has its development and origin based in history, literature, linguistics, sociology, and anthropology; further, each of these fields has adopted its own approach of narrative inquiry. In the past three decades, the use of narrative research has increased in education (predominantly used by teachers to better understand the students' experiences). Psychology has also been warming up to narrative research primarily to understand individuals' personal experiences. An interesting observation is that narrative inquiry is the most commonly used research method in the industry in comparison to the other qualitative research methods. However, it might be true that many professionals may be collecting qualitative data without being aware that they are conducting narrative inquiry/research.

In the previous chapter, I had shared how some quantitative researchers made/make fun of and critique qualitative researchers by saying that qualitative researchers just 'tell stories'. Well, the truth is that telling stories, sharing experiences, and perceptions of the world that we live in is the core of human existence. It is these stories and voices that not only allow us to form an understanding of individuals and communities sharing them but also shed light on the larger structures of the society. These stories tell us about how individuals and communities perceive their identities and what they think of others' perceptions of their identities. Narratives of individuals do not just elucidate individuals' experiences but also their social, cultural, legal, and political position in society.

Narrative inquiry is a powerful method to understand fragments of history through individual experiences. It can enable researchers to get a glimpse of history from perspectives that may not have been officially recorded, known to the larger public, or considered part of the normative historical accounts. Imagine recording the voices of the survivors of the Holocaust, or interacting with families who have lost members in the Holocaust about the memories of these relatives who did not make it. Qualitative researchers have used narrative inquiry to understand the experiences, stories, and voices of individuals who are not present with us today or individuals who are not easily accessible. They do this by talking to their friends, family, other individuals who would have shared experiences with these individuals; or by going through letters, diaries, autobiographies, speeches, pictures or any other artefacts in the public or private domain.

Imagine recording the voices of individuals and families who were separated during the India-Pakistan partition. Imagine talking to your grandparents about how life was for them and their experiences as teenagers – you will not only understand about them but also the society back then from their perspectives. A researcher may also use narrative inquiry over a period of time to capture changes and shifts that have taken place in the narrative.

Narrative inquiry helps us to rehumanise our understanding of the present and history, which may just have been recorded in a very impersonal manner. For instance, the world that we live in today is a post-Covid world. After 10, 20, 50, or 100 years, we will have the numerical data and record for how our world was affected by this pandemic. We will have the global record of the total number of COVID-19 cases, individuals who recovered, individuals who died due to the virus, and individuals who had access to medication and vaccines. However, just numbers will not tell us or the next generations about what the individuals, families and communities went through in different parts of the world during and post the pandemic unless our stories and experiences are recorded. These stories (our stories) will humanise the numbers and statistics related to the pandemic. These stories and experiences will help us tap into the intense emotions and feelings that people have gone through. Hence, as much as narrative inquiry enables us to focus on the historical contexts, it also is an excellent method to focus on situational contexts. The researcher, while doing narrative inquiry, often follows a chronology to make better sense of these situations and historical/present-day/situational contexts, which also allows the researcher in 'restorying' (i.e., reviewing past experiences and narratives in order to have a better understanding of the present and the future).

Though data in narrative research is collected through various tools such as analysis of documents, written work, videos, observations, pictures, artefacts, or any items that trigger and capture memories and experiences., the primary (and also the most commonly used) research tool of narrative research is the interview. Any guesses why? The answer is simple – suppose you had to share a story/experience with someone. The quickest and most convenient way of doing it is by talking (verbally communicating) about these stories/experiences. Do you want to know someone? Talk to them. Do you want to know them better? Talk to them more! And, like mentioned before, if the individual, whose experience you want to record, is not alive or not easily accessible, you can interview and talk to people who would have shared experiences with this individual.

Exercise 4.1 Doing Narrative Research

a) Suppose you were to embark on a research journey with the objective of collecting, recording, and analysing the experiences of Mother Teresa or Mahatma Gandhi through narrative inquiry, what research tools would you use?

b) Suppose you were to conduct qualitative research on a famous person from the 13th century, but you realise that neither this person nor any other individuals who knew this person are alive (duh!). What kind of data will you consider for analysis? From where will you get it? What research tools will you use and, most importantly, will narrative inquiry be the right choice as a research method? Think of someone from the 13th century (Google any person) and make a plan on the way you will approach this research project.

c) Think of three research examples of narrative inquiry's application in social and/or organisational context.

Section 2 – Ethnography

Have you had the opportunity to travel to a culture/society/community different from yours? Or, do you remember the first time when you went to a neighbourhood that felt different from your own even though it was located in the same city? How did it make you feel? What differences and/or similarities did you notice?

Ethnography is a qualitative research method where the researcher observes, interprets, and explains the shared values, beliefs systems, practices, and behaviours of a specific group of people, often referred to as a community (could be a society or even formal and informal organisations, which can be legal or illegal). The focus largely remains on understanding the community's shared and cultural meanings (cultural meaning was explained in Chapter 1). Ethnography is one of the oldest research methods and was initially used by anthropologists to understand communities and societies. In the 19th and 20th century, anthropologists and researchers would go to a distant land – to a community that was very different from theirs – and would conduct 'participant observation' (that is, they would stay with the community, mingle with them to understand their culture, interactions, and the way they function as a community). The early ethnographic studies were criticised for two main reasons:

a. Early ethnographers who went to a faraway unknown land for the study assumed a higher power position that was often reflected in their writing. The point of reference for observing these different cultures was from the stand of the researchers' cultures, which was thought to be superior and more developed. Imagine that you went to an indigenous community and thought that were behind in technology, architecture, and, hence, less developed than you. But, your meaning of development would be influenced by your culture and past experiences (remember the section 'Understanding the meaning of words' in Chapter 1). So, you might end up thinking that the indigenous community is beneath your community/society in terms of what they have achieved (from your standards/parameters of evaluation of achievement). It could be that these communities (which were considered inferior) lived life as it came to them naturally, preferred a different way of life, were forced to choose a different way of life, or were deprived of a better way of life. Whatever may be the reason, the early ethnographers should not have looked down upon the communities. Having a more humanistic approach to doing and writing ethnography will enable you to build rapport with people in the true sense and help you have a reference point where you could view a culture different from yours with lesser judgement.

b. The researcher didn't need to go to an unknown and faraway land/culture. The ethnographic studies could be conducted in the culture/community that the researcher was already a part of, or one that was not completely unknown to the researcher and was in relatively close proximity (at times, distant lands and culture could be more known to the researcher in comparison to the land that the researcher was living in). Following this critique, many researchers started doing interesting ethnographic studies in their communities, or communities that they had relatively higher exposure to. As a result of this, fascinating studies on invisible communities, behaviours, and aspects of society such as crime, poverty, sex work, non-normative gender and sexual identities, and other ignored identities were conducted through the ethnographic method. However, the proximity and accessibility of a community being researched do not always mean that the researcher would be readily accepted by the community.

The state of being out in the field (either in far-off lands or a place close to the researcher) is known as 'fieldwork'. However, the use of the term 'fieldwork' is not just restricted to ethnography but is also used in other methods and research paradigms when the researcher goes out in the field to collect data. The primary data collection tool is participatory observations (we will read about observations as a research tool in the next chapter). The researcher keeps a notebook/diary or digital records of their observations and reflections, commonly referred to as 'field notes'. While doing ethnography, the researcher spends a long time* in the field (done to understand the deeper cultural meanings). Hence, it becomes imperative for the researcher to record their observations and reflections every day, or, at least, at regular intervals, if not every day, to not miss any data points. If you ever take up an ethnographic study, remember to record even data or observations which may feel ordinary to you. While recording the data, the focus should not just be on exceptional or different behaviours, observations, and reflections. There may be many behaviours that come across as usual, basic, uninteresting, or of common sense, but do record them – as ethnographers, you would often be expected to note and present the extraordinary-in-the-ordinary. Recording these ordinary and mundane things/meanings/behaviours of the community will enable you to have richer data and help you in understanding the concealed, hidden, unwritten and unspoken meanings of everyday things. If you feel that some data is not relevant towards the end of the research, you may choose to ignore it, but I cannot lay enough emphasis on having thicker descriptions and observations while recording the data.

Although participatory observation would be your primary data collection tool, consider taking interviews, conducting focused group discussions/conversations, analysing artefacts, or any other tool for data collection while you are in the field. However, remember to first participate and get involved with the community so that they can trust and open up to you. Also, think about how you will or can add value to the community – it is not just about you and your needs to get data and observations for the research. Do not be selfish; think about how you can add value. If you think you cannot add much value, then acknowledge it to yourself first and then to the community – be honest about it and do not promise anything that you cannot live up to, or give false hope to the community about the impact or outcome of the research. As researchers, while staying for an extended period with the community, we can add value in some or the other way (I may be wrong, though). When I say add 'value', I do not mean monetary value or uplifting the community (the community may not need to be uplifted!). Listen to them, smile, offer the gift of music, sing, dance, share food whenever you can with the community, do not be afraid to make a fool of yourself, teach the kids something, help the members of the community with daily tasks (that is, if they want your help and if it is legal), learn their language and history – make some effort (not as a researcher, but as a person who is genuinely interested in the people and their way of life). Stretch yourself and get out of your comfort zone, but keep in mind to not lose yourself. You do not have to pretend to be someone you are not unless you are doing a covert study (more on 'covert study' in Chapter 7). Most importantly, always remember, acknowledge and be grateful that you have the opportunity to study a community. It is the community that adds more value to you and your craft than you can ever add to them.

* How much time is long enough to be in the field while doing ethnographic research?

The time taken for ethnographic study depends mainly on the research objective and if you, as a researcher, feel that you have been successful in understanding and capturing the values, beliefs, and cultural meanings of the community being studied. There have been researchers who have spent years with the community. The time spent in the field also depends on the researcher's ability to build rapport and be accepted by the community. However, not all factors are under the researcher's control while building rapport – some factors such as race, ethnicity, nationality, and gender of the researcher impact the process. There may be other factors related to resources such as the funding available for the study and the time allotted to finish the study (academic or client-related deadline) that also impacts the overall period that a researcher can spend doing fieldwork. Researchers' requirement to spend an extended period in the field is the main reason for corporates and industries to avoid the adoption of ethnographic methods. Most businesses today desire fast-moving research (thanks to the VUCA world we live in).

To uncomplicate things for you, if at all I would have to suggest a specific duration for ethnographic studies, it would be 18 months, especially while researching regional communities defined by geographical boundaries. Any guesses why? (Try to think – remember, anything you do in research needs to follow reason.) A period of 18 months would be ideal because, for the first year (12 months), you will be able to observe one complete cycle. Different communities have different rituals and behave differently during different times of the year. In these 12 months, you will observe different occasions, festivals, rituals, and celebrations that take place in a year's cycle. In the remaining six months, the objective would be to see if you get similar observations compared to the first six months of the research. If there are no significant differences during this time, congratulations – your data may have reached saturation to some extent (data saturation is achieved when you start getting similar data and observing similar patterns over time). However, unless you are doing your PhD (or you are a free bird far from the expectations of society, have a love for qualitative research, are naturally curious to know new people and culture, and have some money in your bank), you may not be able to spend so much time doing ethnography. While doing an ethnographic study in the organisational context, the time you will spend in the field (that is, in the organisation) will be much less. This will largely depend on your responsibilities and time commitment to other stakeholders and clients (if at all they agree to an ethnographic approach). I often tell my master's students to take ethnographic study in organisational set-ups during their summer break/internships even though it is barely for two months just to get a taste of what it is like to be an ethnographer, and because there is limited ethnographic literature in the organisational context. It is only when more ethnographic studies/projects are conducted in organisational set-ups that organisations will realise the true potential of this qualitative research method. Remember, when you think that ethnography is the right method for the research, but you do not have the time, consult your research guide/client and attempt to do it in whatever time you have and write reasons for your inability to spend extended periods in the field as your research limitation (most researchers will understand).

Insider and outsider perspective: In most early ethnographic studies, when the researcher went to a distant land/community for research, the researcher would often enter as an outsider. During fieldwork, the researcher would attempt to understand the community and be accepted and recognised as one of the community members. A researcher who would go as an outsider to the community would strive to become an insider as it would mean that people from the community could share their lives with the researcher as they would share it with another member of the community. However, it is not always the case that the researcher enters the community as an outsider during the initial phase of the study. When a researcher conducts ethnographic research in a community that they are already part of or with a community that is not distinct from their own, the chances of being considered an insider even during the initial phase of the research is higher. It might even be possible that the researcher goes in as an insider but comes out as an outsider. This happens when, after spending time with the community, either the community does not think the researcher to be one of their own or the researcher does not relate to the community. Broadly speaking, four outcomes are possible:

a. The researcher goes into the community as an outsider – and comes out as an insider.
b. The researcher goes into the community as an outsider – and remains an outsider.
c. The researcher goes into the community as an insider – and comes out as an outsider.
d. The researcher goes into the community as an insider – and remains an insider.

But, who decides if the researcher is an outsider or insider?

The relationship that a researcher builds with the community while doing an ethnographic study is like most other relationships – where both the researcher and the community play an important role in deciding the researcher's position within the community. But, I would still say that it is primarily the community that decides the researcher's position and placement (which changes over time depending on the interactions that the researcher has with the community).

What is good – being an insider or an outsider?

As an insider, the researcher already knows a lot about the community and can dive into deeper shared meanings quickly. However, when the researcher is an outsider, they bring a fresh set of eyes and can observe even mundane or everyday things, which may be taken for granted and/or go unseen/unnoticed from an insider perspective. The reference point of making cultural comparisons would be different for both, a researcher writing from an insider perspective as compared to one writing from an outsider perspective, and both these reference points are important to understand the community being researched.

Though most people would think that being an insider is an advantage over being an outsider, both perspectives have their own set of advantages, as discussed above. **What is good and important is that a researcher is accepted by the community. You must understand that when I say the researcher is 'accepted', I do not mean that the researcher is considered an insider (though there is an overlap between being accepted and being an insider). What I mean is that the researcher is accepted by the community either as an insider or an outsider.** There may be times when a researcher is accepted and included by the community but is not considered an insider. This is possible when the community being researched acknowledges and is tolerant towards the researcher's values, belief systems, and subjective meanings that are different from that of the community. Hence, the focus of the researcher should be to be 'accepted' to be able to conduct research.

Autoethnography: Now, we have seen that in an ethnographic study, the focus, while doing the fieldwork, is a community or organisation. The researcher strives to understand the culture, values, belief systems, and behaviours of the community. Although autoethnography is similar to ethnographic research in terms of the process of recording observations and interpreting data, the focus of the researcher is on observing the interaction of the self with the social structures of the society and vice-versa. In ethnographic research, the community is at the centre of the study. In contrast, in an autoethnographic study, it is the researcher who becomes the centre of the study. Due to this focus of autoethnographic research, the researcher aims to understand how the self interacts and perceives society, and, at the same time, how the society interacts and perceives the researcher's identities. Further, the focus is also on how these interactions influence the researcher's worldview, perceptions, behaviours, and subjective meanings. The researcher tries to achieve these interactions with the society by rigorously recording their personal experiences and reflections. Autoethnography is an autobiography but following the rigour of observations and fieldwork of ethnography.

Exercise 4.2: It's time to do some ethnography

This exercise would take a relatively long time, higher commitment, and discipline with recording

---

observations regularly.

Think of a place that is easily accessible to you. This could be a place you are currently visiting. It could be your school, college, workplace, your gym (if you are regular at your gym), a club, an NGO, or even a place of worship. You can choose any place, but remember that you need to regularly visit this place, so choosing a place that is already integrated into your daily schedule will help. Attempt doing an ethnographic study in these places. Record your observation regularly on things such as ethics, values, and normative behaviours along with the collective and cultural meaning attached by the people accessing it. Also, focus on the activities which are mundane/regular to get to the extraordinary-in-the-ordinary.

Decide on a time frame when you would want to spend doing this exercise – the objective is to get a taste of what it is like to do ethnography (if not ethnography, then, at least, extended participatory observations).

If you plan to build a qualitative research portfolio, I highly recommend doing this exercise with an NGO or community business. In case you cannot venture out or do not have access to a physical space for an extended period, try doing this exercise in a virtual space/community. Individuals who want to make a career in social media research,

UX research, and digital humanities should also try a digital ethnography project. You can apply the same instructions in digital spaces with virtual communities. It could be a social media/networking platform that has virtual communities. Try observing people participating in these virtual groups/communities, what their profile tells about them, what behaviours they display online, how they interact with other individuals from the community, what ethics, values, and norms are prevalent in this digital community.

Section 3 – Case Study Method

The case study method is a relatively newer method of qualitative research and is widely gaining popularity, especially in higher education. Individuals who have studied management at an undergraduate or graduate level would have been exposed to many cases. Case study, as a method, is used in qualitative research when the researcher wants to focus on a particular unit of analysis (case) or multiple units of analysis (multiple cases – when presenting a comparative case analysis). Here, the unit of analysis could be a person, an organisation (entity/group of people that have some shared goals), or an event(s) (actions that lead to an event). Although most cases would feature all units of analysis – a person, organisation, or event(s) – the primary focus is mostly on only one of these units. Let us understand this with a few examples:

a) In 2012, there was labour unrest at the Maruti Suzuki automobile manufacturing plant located in Manesar, India, which resulted in an HR executive's death and left many employees injured. If qualitative research was to be conducted to explore the incident, what would be the primary unit of analysis – a person (the HR executive who was murdered), an organisation/group of people (in this case, it could be the labour union, the management or the entire organisation, i.e. Maruti), or an event/series of events that lead to violence and killing at the workplace? Here, the primary unit of analysis will be the event or series of events that led to violence, leaving an employee dead and several others injured. The people and organisations will be the secondary units of analysis while writing the case.

b) Suppose you want to conduct a case study on exponential start-ups (start-ups that are growing exponentially compared to their competitors/other start-ups in the same field) to understand why some start-ups are more successful and have an accelerated growth rate. What will be your primary unit of analysis? In this case, it should be organisations/entities.

Exercise 4.3

Just like the above examples, think of three real-life examples where the primary unit of analysis of the case is 'person/individual'.

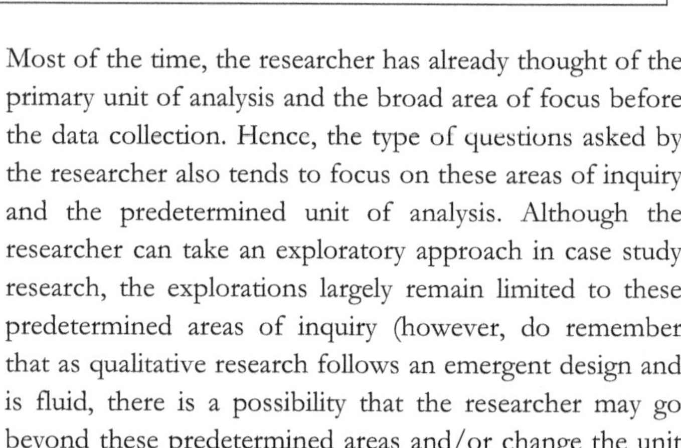

Most of the time, the researcher has already thought of the primary unit of analysis and the broad area of focus before the data collection. Hence, the type of questions asked by the researcher also tends to focus on these areas of inquiry and the predetermined unit of analysis. Although the researcher can take an exploratory approach in case study research, the explorations largely remain limited to these predetermined areas of inquiry (however, do remember that as qualitative research follows an emergent design and is fluid, there is a possibility that the researcher may go beyond these predetermined areas and/or change the unit of analysis while collecting data, given that these changes follow substantial reasoning and are more appropriate in fulfilling the research objectives).

The most commonly used research tools in the case study method are interviews, focused group discussions, and analysis of documents/literature relevant to the case. The researcher has a negligible role or influence over the participants' behaviours or the outcome of the case. The case study method has a very journalistic style of gathering data – just like journalists collect evidence relevant to the case, researchers also focus on collecting the relevant responses and data. The focus while reporting and disseminating the study is mainly on the contemporary issues or topics of the recent past and less on historical events. Historical data is included only to the extent it helps the researcher in setting up the context/premise of the case and/or when historical data has some progression/influence over the events that lead to the case.

Section 4 - Phenomenology

Have you ever gone through a break-up? If yes, how did it feel? Can you describe the feeling in detail? If you have not experienced a break-up yet, then lucky you (however, someday, you will :P)!

How did you feel at the time when you or your partner broke up?

Was this feeling the same after six months or maybe a year? How did it change over time, and if there was a change, what was the reason behind it? Were you able to move on and get over the relationship? I have had my share of heartbreaks. I have seen many of my friends going through heartbreaks. I have stayed in hostels during my master's and PhD, and whenever a friend went through a break-up, the norm was to accompany them to drinking sessions – they drink and share their pain with you (which may come across as repetitive and irrational over few sessions), while you act as the responsible one and ensure that the friend reaches back to the hostel. The initial phase of a break-up is mostly denial, followed by the truth walloping you while you attempt to get over the feeling through various coping mechanisms (some of the ways to cope up popularised by media is alcohol, rebound relationships, or even taking the 'walk of shame' after sleeping with random people!). And finally, after some time, you will perhaps be able to accept the truth and move on. So, if I were to ask you to tell me the essence or meaning of a break-up in its purest form, what would you say? I know it is difficult to put in words what an individual goes through during heartbreak, but still, if you were to try to explain the meaning of a break-up consciously, what would you say, I wonder!

Phenomenology is a qualitative research method where the researcher attempts to understand the essence of the meaning (maybe in the purest form) of a lived experience. Apart from understanding the essence, the objective of phenomenological research can also be to compare it with similar kinds of experiences. For instance, break-ups are often followed by the separation of lovers. But, separation is a larger phenomenon and takes place not just in romantic relationships but also in other kinds of relationships. An individual may separate from friends, families, or other living and non-living things close to them. As a researcher doing a phenomenological study, you may want to compare separations in different situations and contexts. Commonly, phenomenological research attempts to study various individuals' lived experiences to understand the universal meaning behind a phenomenon.

If I had to further simplify phenomenology, I would say that the researchers attempt to understand individuals' experiences through a particular psychological and physiological journey. Often phenomenological research tries to answer questions such as 'What is it like to go through a certain experience?', 'How does it feel to go through a certain experience?', 'How is the feeling of a certain experience compared to the feeling of other similar experiences?', 'What is the universal meaning attached by various individuals going through similar phenomena?', etc.

Transcendental and Hermeneutic Phenomenology: There have been developments within the phenomenological literature, which has led to different types of phenomenological approaches. The manner in which phenomenology is to be conducted or even defined will be different for phenomenologists belonging to different schools of thought. The two main developments (or types of phenomenology) are transcendental and hermeneutic phenomenology, coined by Edmund Husserl and Martin Heidegger respectively (by the way, Heidegger was Husserl's student, who disagreed with Husserl's way of understanding and doing phenomenology and came up with a new type). The approach suggested by Husserl is the traditional school of thought that emphasises bracketing, which means that an individual is supposed to keep aside their biases while attempting to understand the phenomenon. In transcendental phenomenology, the focus is on 'phenomenological reduction' – a process of intentional bracketing to understand the phenomenon's pure essence. If you ever want to bracket your biases while doing transcendental phenomenology, remember the following:

a) Do not assume things or take meaning for granted – go with a fresh set of eyes (figuratively).

b) Be critical even of the meanings of things that are considered obvious, and question these meanings.

c) Continuous questioning (of the answers to the same question) will help you to reach closer to the pure form of meaning – so, question and re-question.

d) Keep a check on the unsaid and unwritten norms and behaviours as this will help you know if you are conforming to the expected behaviour of the society (as a researcher, you are required to stay neutral). For instance, assume that you are doing phenomenological research on 'what does it feel like to be in physical pain', and, as part of the research, you meet a person who has recently broken a leg in an accident. As a larger cultural norm, you are expected to show concern, empathise, ask the person how the accident happened, and if things would be better soon. It would be considered rude in most cultures to tell this person that you are happy that they broke their leg, or to not empathise or express your concern for the person in pain. However, there are times when our behaviours are not considered appropriate by the larger society. Have you ever laughed at a person who slipped and fell in front of you when the larger culture has taught you to help the person in distress? Or, have you seen a video being forwarded/shared as a 'funny video' that shows some person getting hurt? Most of us have laughed at such videos where a person in pain or distress.

e) The act of critical re-questioning (so that you don't make assumptions and stay neutral in transcendental phenomenology) may come across as an interrogation or a rude gesture to the participants. It is not expected social behaviour.

However, this can be addressed by explaining and sensitising the participants about the process and methodology before collecting data.

As already mentioned, Heidegger was not convinced of Husserl's underlying philosophy of bracketing. His conflict was that it would not be possible for an individual to keep aside their assumptions and biases completely, and be critical and question at all times to get to the essence of a phenomenon. Hence, Heidegger believed that individuals should recognise their biases and interpret an experience or the phenomenon that is being studied while acknowledging the natural process of attaching meaning and interpretations. Hence, in hermeneutic phenomenology, the researcher can use other lenses to understand the phenomena, which is not possible with transcendental phenomenology. For instance, a researcher may try to understand an experience or a phenomenon using a framework such as the Feminist framework or the Marxist framework. Using different frameworks is not allowed in transcendental phenomenology as the emphasis is on getting rid of any preconceived assumptions/perceptions through bracketing.

The most common research tools used in phenomenology to collect data are interviews, observations, focused group discussions, and diary studies. Though phenomenology is one of the oldest qualitative research methods, it is one of the least used − primarily because of its philosophical nature, which makes it difficult to understand and even more challenging to implement while doing research. I hope that I was able to simplify the concept of phenomenology to some extent without losing the true essence/pure meaning of what phenomenological research is (see what I did there? :P).

> **Reading recommendation:** If the complexity of phenomenology is something that you are attracted to and want to read more to gain a better understanding, go through the amazing resource on Phenomenology at Stanford Encyclopedia of Philosophy (reference and link below).
>
> Smith, David Woodruff, "Phenomenology", *The Stanford Encyclopedia of Philosophy* (Summer 2018 Edition), Edward N. Zalta (ed.), URL = <https://plato.stanford.edu/archives/sum2018/entries/phenomenology/>.
>
> Practitioners and students who would want to explore phenomenological research in an organisational context can read the following paper.
>
> Tomkins, L. and Eatough, V. (2013), "The feel of experience: phenomenological ideas for organisational research", *Qualitative Research in Organisations and Management*, Vol. 8 No. 3, pp. 258-275. https://doi.org/10.1108/QROM-04-2012-1060

Section 5 – Grounded Theory Method

The Grounded Theory Method was discovered in 1967 by Barney Glaser and Anselm Strauss. Its primary objective is to introduce new social sciences theories and/or verify previous theories, assumptions, and generalisations. It is based on the foundation of constant comparison of data and theoretical sampling.

Constant comparison of data and theoretical sampling: Suppose you have some assumptions/belief systems based on your previous experience, knowledge, and worldview and think it has the potential to be verified and validated as a theory in social sciences. So, with this objective in mind, you take up qualitative research using grounded theory as a research method. What you want to do now is collect data from various individuals/communities and sources that will enable you to conclude towards the end of the research if a theory emerges from the data (theory grounded in data). You meet your first participant/community and collect data from them using various research tools – let us call this your 'first data point'. Now, you will analyse the 'first data point', which would inform you if there is a possibility of theory emerging from the data. However, just your 'first data point' is an inadequate sample. You would need to collect more data to achieve data saturation – a state when you start observing similar patterns from various data points for the theory to be accepted. Hence, you now go to the 'second data point' to collect data. Once you have successfully collected data from the 'second data point', you first analyse it and then compare it with the 'first data point' to note similarities and differences in the two data points. Then, proceed to the 'third data point'. Once you have collected data from the 'third data point', you analyse it, compare it with the first and the second data points. You keep continuing this process – where you collect data from a new data point and then compare it with the previous data set. This is known as the constant comparison of data in grounded theory. You stop collecting data when the data reaches saturation (you will see various patterns emerging that will lead to the theory). As a researcher, your focus, while selecting the sample at each stage, would be guided by the objective of establishing or negating a theory, also known as theoretical sampling. For instance, in the initial phase, you collect data points from 'City A', and you note the similarities and differences in the sample, and conclude with a theory. But, then you might not sure if the theory holds for a different city or a different culture. So, you then collect various data points from 'City B' and compare them to that of 'City A'. Hence, the decision related to the sample in grounded theory would be based on the objective of strengthening or negating a theory. When the researcher is sure that the theory would emerge and stay true for a population with specific characteristics, they may want to test the theory with a population which has different characteristics (to note if the theory holds across populations with distinct characteristics). Hence, due to theoretical sampling in grounded theory, the sampling follows an emergent and fluid design.

While using other research methods in qualitative research, the researcher generally starts with a literature review. However, while using grounded theory research, the researcher directly starts with the data collection process (any guesses why?). This is primarily because exposure to previous literature may colour how the researcher views and thinks about the theory that is to be tested and verified. Further, it may influence the researcher's interpretation and arguments for strengthening and/or negating theories. Whenever I tell my students that, in a grounded theory method, the research does not begin with a review of literature, they become thrilled (thinking one less thing to do while doing a research project). However, it is to be noted that the researcher does a review of literature after analysing and synthesising the data from the field, so the literature review takes place towards the end of the research process rather than at the beginning. It may so happen that the researcher comes up with a theory after the data analysis only to realise (during the literature review) that there is already a similar theory. If this happens, the researcher should not worry – in fact, it further validates the theory (the known knowledge) and makes it more relevant. There may be a theory that says something opposite to what you are proposing. Again, nothing to worry about – in such situations, the researcher should aim to understand the previous theory's framework, compare, critique, and add to the existing knowledge. A researcher may also introduce a new theory that is not found in previous literature (but the researcher would still have to do a literature review to know that the theory proposed by them does not exist).

Exercise 4.4: In a sentence

Just in one sentence, write when the following research methods are used. Remember that the researcher needs to know the reason behind selecting each of the methods. The researcher cannot randomly select a method. In case you find it difficult to explain in one sentence when a particular research method is used, reread that section in this chapter. Even after rereading it, if you still find it difficult to explain when a research

---

method is used, refer to the cheat sheet at the end of this book.

E.g. Narrative inquiry is used when the research objective is to <u>explore, record and understand the voices, experiences, and stories of people.</u>

Now, it is your turn.

The case study method is used when the research objective is to:

Phenomenology is used when the research objective is to:

Ethnography is used when the research objective is to:

Grounded Theory Method is used when the research objective is to:

Congratulate yourself and give yourself a treat – you now know the basics of the five most commonly used qualitative research methods.

CHAPTER 5
RESEARCH TOOLS

Hope you remember me going on and on about how research methods and tools are different from each other in the last chapter. We discussed that research tools are used under research methods to collect data. Some research tools are better suited to certain research methods. For instance, if your research method is the narrative inquiry, then the primary research tools should enable you to listen and record participants' voices (these will be tools such as interviews and focus group discussions). In this chapter, we will be going through some of the most commonly used research tools in qualitative research. Let us begin!

Section 1 – Interviews

An interview is a research tool where the researcher (interviewer) has a conversation with the participant with the objective of collecting their experiences, understanding perceptions and opinions, and recording voices. At times, an interview is used as a tool to know about the perceptions or experiences of another individual to whom the researcher does not have direct access. The most commonly used types of interviews are structured, semi-structured, and unstructured interviews. There are other classifications/types (refer to Table 5.1), but know that there is an overlap between there classifications (for example, a structured interview can also be a virtual interview done with an expert).

Table 5.1. Common typology/classification of the interview:

Classification based on the fluidity the researcher has in going beyond the interview schedule	• Structured interviews (sticks to the question in the interview schedule) • Semi-structured interviews (some flexibility with regard to the researcher asking questions outside the interview schedule, but largely in the relevant areas) • Unstructured interviews (more like a free-flowing conversation; highest fluidity with respect to the direction the discussion takes place)
Classification based on the place where the interview is conducted	• Face-to-face interviews • Remote or virtual interviews (can be with video, or only audio, or telephonic interviews)
Classification based on the profile of the participant	• Expert interviews • High-profile interviews • General interviews

Before deep-diving into these classifications, let us

understand what an interview schedule is.

Interview Schedule: It is a set of questions or broad themes that the researcher can refer to while conducting the interview. I do not have a sharp memory, so I often prepare and carry the interview schedule with me (even when the interview is unstructured). It acts as a guide and a checklist that I can refer to during the interview and ensure that I cover all important areas. Further, it enables me to be consistent with the questions and/or areas of discussion while interviewing many participants for the research. Often, in qualitative market research, there may be many researchers simultaneously conducting interviews at multiple locations. In such a situation, where more than one researcher is collecting data, an interview schedule helps the researchers to be consistent while collecting data from several participants. If you are a researcher in the industry, you will often be required to share the interview schedule with the clients or relevant stakeholders before commencing data collection.

Note: The researcher conducting the interview may be referred to as an interviewer, or simply as the researcher. The person being interviewed for the research is commonly known as the participant (at times, they may also be referred to as the interviewee). You may have heard the terms 'interviewer' and 'interviewee' before in the context of the recruitment/admission process. However, note that an interview's objective for a job or the selection/rejection of a candidate is different from that of research. While doing research interviews, remember that you are not judging the person; instead, you are interested in their stories and experiences.

Interview classification based on fluidity: Depending on the liberty a researcher has to go beyond the questions/areas/themes of the interview schedule, the interviews can be classified as structured, semi-structured, and unstructured. This means that during a structured interview, the researcher sticks to the interview schedule, which is mostly extensive in nature. Structured interviews are often conducted when the researcher has absolute clarity on the questions to be asked and wants to keep the scope of the research within the predefined objectives. An example of this would be a specific goal-oriented qualitative market research where the organisation wants to develop and test concepts for their product communication. The researcher will conduct user/non-user interviews and get detailed qualitative feedback on the concepts. Another example could be a qualitative advertisement or storyboard evaluation. In both, the client or the stakeholders would not be interested in exploratory research findings or insights that are beyond the predetermined scope. Further, the parameters for evaluating these research projects would be predetermined.

However, it is to be noted that not asking questions beyond the interview schedule, even when structured interviews are used as a tool, should not be treated as the only way of going about it. If, as a researcher, you feel that asking an unplanned question would help to capture reality better, feel free to do it (remember, one of the primary essences of qualitative research is fluidity). However, if you observe yourself diverting from the interview schedule too many times, you may want to change your research tool from a structured interview to a semi-structured interview, or you can revisit the current interview schedule to populate it further with relevant questions.

Unstructured interviews are exactly the opposite of structured interviews. It has the most fluidity when compared to other interview tools. In fact, the fluidity in an unstructured interview is so high with respect to what questions are to be asked that the researcher may not even have predetermined questions for the participants. However, it is advisable to have broad themes even while not having specific questions (themes are broad areas of inquiry). Unstructured interviews are a great tool when the researcher is in the exploratory phase of the research or conducting exploratory research. Further, many researchers use unstructured interviews especially when the research is of a sensitive nature. Imagine that a participant is sharing some personal issues with you, and instead of having an approach that allows them to feel comfortable and share more, you adamantly follow a structured set of questions. The participant will most likely not feel comfortable sharing their personal experiences. Hence, especially when the research is on a sensitive issue or issues that can be very personal to the participants, unstructured interviews can be a more humanistic tool for listening and capturing data. Having an unstructured interview enables the data collection process to be led by the conversation of the participants rather than the predetermined questions that the researcher may have.

Semi-structured interviews are somewhere between structured and unstructured interviews. The researcher often has a set of predetermined questions, but also there is room to go beyond and explore areas that are not covered in the interview schedule. When my students are not sure of which type of interview to use for the data collection process, I tell them to begin with semi-structured interviews. Later, when they have conducted a couple of interviews, they can judge if the research needs more focused questions (a structured interview technique), a more fluid approach (an unstructured interview technique), or they would like some room for exploration while having a set interview schedule (a semi-structured interview).

Classification based on the place where the interview is conducted: The interviews may be face-to-face or could be done remotely. In face-to-face interviews, the researcher has a higher scope of observing the participants' overall reaction. As qualitative researchers, even when the primary focus is on recording the experiences of the participants through interviews, we should take notes on the participants' vocal modulation (tone, pitch, stress, and rate of speech), facial expressions, and body language. Suppose you are interviewing a participant and the participant takes much longer to respond to a particular question as compared to the previous questions does this silence mean anything, and can you interpret it? Can silence also have some meanings attached to it?

While it is possible to record fluctuations in the voice and facial expressions through video calls, it does not allow the researcher to capture the complete body language. If the researcher is conducting a telephonic conversation, then they do not have access to both facial expressions and body language as data points. Suppose a researcher is researching on and needs to talk to a person of colour to record their experiences through a telephonic interview. The researcher will have to confirm with the participant during this conversation if they are a person of colour as, unlike in a face-to-face interview or a video call, they would not have access to visual cues. However, remote interviews (through video calls or telephonic interviews) allow the researcher to cover vast geographical distances, offer higher flexibility, and can be less expensive than face-to-face interviews.

Classifications based on the participant's profile: Interviews can also be classified on the basis of the participant that is being interviewed. The three broad categories are expert interviews, high-profile interviews, and general interviews. As the name suggests, **expert interviews** are conducted with experts in a specific field. For instance, if you are researching mental health issues, apart from talking to participants from different cohorts, you shall also talk to experts working in the area of mental health. These experts may be practising doctors, psychologists, psychiatrists, academicians, and social workers. The experts would have comprehensive knowledge in their areas of specialisation. You can interview them to gain in-depth micro and systems-level understanding. It is advisable that in most cases, before meeting the expert, you go through previous literature to be able to ask more relevant questions. Often, the expert interviews might guide your research design and process; hence, do conduct an expert interview before starting your research with the participants. You may also want to meet the expert in the analysis phase (once the data is collected) to get their interpretation of some of the findings.

Getting access to an expert is difficult, so make the most of the time you have with them. If you can build a rapport with an expert, then nothing like it – you may get access to candid opinions and experiences of the expert. From my experience, the best way of getting these candid opinions is to not meet the expert at their workplace (a semi-formal restaurant or café that is less crowded is better). You will receive the most interesting data from the expert when they are speaking off-the-record after the official interview is over. Do account for some extra time for these informal conversations while planning the expert interview.

High-profile interviews are similar to expert interviews. High-profile individuals may or may not be an expert in their field (but the likelihood that they would be an expert is pretty high). It is difficult to reach out and fix appointments with most high-profile individuals. If your research includes interacting or taking interviews of such individuals, then you may want to account for a longer time for their recruitment. However, it is likely that you will not be able to achieve data saturation because you may not be able to conduct enough units (number) of interviews to draw patterns from your data. Getting access to one high-profile individual is difficult in the first place. Hence, to be able to do enough interviews to reach data saturation is challenging. Do not worry if you cannot reach data saturation with high-profile individuals; however, do mention this as your research limitation.

If you are lucky and manage to get an appointment with high-profile individuals, do plan your interview schedule well to make the most of the limited time you get with them. There is a possibility that the high-profile individual (or their manager/PR) may want to see your interview schedule in advance. They may have other instructions as well for you with respect to recording and disseminating the data. Even when there are no such instructions, ensure that you have a written communication around the use of the information that you gather from them and the way the same would be represented in the research (to avoid conflicts later). You may have to reveal the identity of these individuals, especially when the research is to be commercially disseminated in the form of a book or a documentary. If you are ever in such a position, ensure that you have written consent from these individuals on revealing their identities (as a general norm, researchers do not reveal their participants' identity – you will read more on this in Chapter 7).

In case you are not able to find individuals for a high-profile interview, change your strategy. You can try and get people who would have interacted and spent time with these individuals. If that is not possible either, then you may want to check if these high-profile individuals share their thoughts on social media platforms or if their speeches or interviews are available online. You can use these as data and analyse them for your research. It will be nothing like talking to these individuals in person, but you would have some access to their thoughts and works (thank you, internet). One of my students wanted to qualitatively study the similarities between the leadership styles of Donald Trump and Narendra Modi. Now, this student did not have access to interviews and observations directly, so she decided to analyse the information available on the internet including speeches given by both the leaders in various forums and their opinions and expressions on social media platforms such as Twitter! Due to the internet, we now have access to at least some of these high-profile individuals' virtual identities!

For the lack of a better term, interviews conducted with different types of people from all walks of life are known as general interviews, or simply referred to as interviews. However, do keep in mind that not all types of people from our daily lives may be easily visible and accessible to us as researchers. Do not treat participants of general interviews any less than participants who are experts or high-profile. Do not think that they are ordinary. Remember that most people come across as ordinary until we hear their extraordinary experiences and stories. For a qualitative researcher, each participant is unique irrespective of their background and status in society.

Types of questions asked in an interview (open, close, and leading questions): I have seen many new qualitative researchers (most of my students in the initial days asking close-ended questions. There have been times when I have seen interview schedules with mostly close-ended questions and one or two open-ended questions at the end. This primarily happens because we have mostly filled survey forms with close-ended questions in our lives and various spaces of society. You would have come across close-ended questions/surveys post dining at the restaurant, ordering products online, booking your travel tickets, availing service, or buying a product. There might be few open-ended questions in these surveys asking you about your experience in detail, but you would have skipped those or given half-hearted answers (who wants to write so much in these forms anyway!). There are some exceptions when you treat these open-ended questions with more respect – when these are part of your college or job applications. However, if people choose not to write those long answers or those mentally draining college essays or give a written explanation of why an employer should hire them, most people would skip it!

Remember, if you are doing qualitative research and your interview schedule has more close-ended questions than open-ended ones, it no longer remains a qualitative interview schedule – it becomes a quantitative survey! But, what are open and close-ended questions? Close-ended questions give the participants predetermined options as answers. Here are some examples of close-ended questions:

- How are you feeling today?
  a)   Good   b) Not so good

- How are you feeling today? (Select one of the following options)
  a)   Excellent
  b)   b) Good
  c)   c) Okay
  d)   b) Not so good
  e)   e) Don't even ask me!

- On a scale of 1 to 5 (with 1 being the lowest score and 5 being the highest score), how are you feeling today?
  a) 1
  b) 2
  c) 3
  d) 4
  e) 5

- How are you feeling today?
  a) :)   b) :0   c) :(

All of the above are examples of close-ended questions. In this set, the question is the same, but the options given to the participants are different (I have done this to show you how the same close-ended question can have different types of options).

So, what is an open-ended question? Open-ended questions give the participants a greater degree of freedom to express themselves as it does not have predetermined options. So, the question 'How are you feeling today?' without any options will be open-ended. It might so happen that a researcher asks the participant an open-ended question, but the participant reverts with only one or two words, for example:

Researcher: How are you feeling today?

Participant: Good

In the above example, we can see that the participant has answered the question with only one word – 'Good'. If the participant is not expressive, the researcher may have to ask more questions to make the most of these open-ended questions. Most of the time, you will get more elaborate responses by asking 'Why'.

Researcher: How are you feeling today?

Participant: Good

Research: Why are you feeling good?

Participant: I finished writing a book. I have been working on it for a very long time, and finally, I did it.

In the above conversation, you will note that asking 'Why' leads the participant to elaborate on their response. While doing qualitative research, the researchers need to get thick descriptions. So, whenever you feel that you could have a more detailed response from the participant, ask them 'Why'. But, you need not do this for every question. Some will only be warm-up questions that are meant to build rapport with the participants. So, decide which questions are important and where you would like to dive deep. For instance, 'How are you feeling today?' can be a warm-up question or just a greeting (question asked out of courtesy. But the same 'How are you feeling today?' can be an important probe area when researching mental or physical health issues. So, the context and research objective will help you determine the questions that you have to get thick or detailed responses to. It is not that a researcher never asks close-ended questions while doing qualitative research, but remember that most of your questions have to be open-ended. An open-ended question is only as good as the researcher's ability to obtain a detailed response from the participant.

Leading questions: A leading question is when the researcher leads or influences the participant to answer in a certain way. For instance, when the researcher asks the participant, 'How are you feeling today?', the researcher is not influencing how the participant will answer the question. But, if the researcher asks the participant 'Tell me something that made you feel good today?', 'Tell me something good about today', 'What made you feel bad today?', or 'Are you feeling good today?', they become leading questions. Further, the level of influence will defer to the way the question is structured. In the question 'What made you feel good today?', the participant has a limited scope of saying about how they are feeling or the bad things that they might have felt. Most of the time, the participant is forced to respond with a focus on 'feeling good'. Compare the question 'What made you feel good today?' with 'Are you feeling good today?', and you will realise that the second question, though a leading question, still gives the participant some flexibility of saying that they may not be feeling good. Conversely, 'Tell me your experience of using the product' – this is not a leading question as the participant can share whatever is on their mind post the product usage. But, 'Tell me something that you like about the product usage experience' or 'Tell me something that you did not like about the product usage experience' are leading questions.

Both leading and non-leading questions are used in qualitative research. However, ensure that your initial questions are non-leading. This will help you to know what is naturally present for the participants. Post that, you can use leading questions to get focused answers in specific areas. For instance, while getting qualitative product feedback from the participants, first ask them about their overall experience. This will enable the participant to share what they felt after using the product. They may share good or bad experiences. Then, you can focus on getting further details on what was good and bad about the product through leading questions. Avoid starting the interview with leading questions, that way, you will first come to know what is on top of the mind of the participant and not influence their responses.

Exercise 5.1: Write that interview schedule

Your friend has realised their true calling in life. They want to quit their job to become a full-time pet photographer. But, before taking this step of leaving a financially stable job, they want to ensure that they are not just thinking with their heart but also with the mind (objectively). They need your help. They want you to talk to a few pet owners about their perceptions and expectations from a professional pet photography service. You have agreed to help your friend. Before interviewing pet owners, you now have to make an interview schedule   .

- What type of interview schedule will you construct – structured, semi-structured, or unstructured?
- What is the reason behind you choosing a specific kind of interview schedule over others?

Once you have decided the kind of interview that you will proceed with, you now have to prepare the interview schedule. Write the questions that you

---

would be asking the pet owners.

Towards the end of this book, I have attached a sample interview schedule. Go through it after you have written your interview schedule because if you see my interview schedule first, you may think in the way that I have thought. That way, we will not be able to see the similarities and differences between both our interview schedules. Also, feel free to critique and improve the interview schedule that I have attached. Try to make it better – think of the questions/areas of investigation that I might have missed and add them to the interview schedule.

Section 2 – Focus Group Discussion (FGD)

Focus Group Discussions (FGD) are similar to interviews – where the objective is to know the participants' experiences, voices, and perceptions about a certain reality in a group setting. However, the number of participants in an FGD ranges from four to eight individuals, in contrast to interviews where, mostly, there is one participant. There are no defined rules concerning how many participants should be included in one FGD; however, it is advisable to not have more than 10 participants in one group so that you can capture the voices of all the participants. The participants gather for an FGD to discuss a common subject or a shared experience (imagine that you are conducting an FGD and all the participants are talking about different things – the discussion would be a mess). So, often, the topic of the FGD remains common for all the participants, and the researcher plays the role of a facilitator, thus, guiding the discussion.

I have often seen that when an FGD is conducted, the researcher asks the participants a question, and each participant reverts to the researcher, taking turns. FGDs, then, become a question-and-answer session with the researcher whereas it should be a discussion. Apart from collecting the narrative of the participants, the objective of conducting an FDG is also to note the interactions that take place among the participants. Does every participant agree with each other on everything they say? Does any participant change their view after hearing out other participants? Does a participant become more adamant on their stance? As a researcher, you should observe the group dynamics and how it changes over the course of the FGD. The researcher should not become the centre of the discussion; instead, the researcher should guide and facilitate the discussion. One of the simplest ways of achieving this is by making the participants sit in a circle. Sitting on one side with the participants facing you will only reinforce that you are higher in the power dynamics and that the participants are supposed to talk to you. Hence, it is best if the researcher sits with the participants in the circle to be seen as one of them. The discussion and exchange among the participants are of a higher degree, leading to better group dynamics. If the FGD is conducted virtually, ensure that the participants have not pinned your screen and that they can see all the participants. I will not advise conducting an FGD without a video (only audio FGD) as communicating will become difficult for the participants without the visual cues (due to multiple individuals involved in the conversation). Further, in such scenarios, the research would lose important non-verbal observations.

While conducting an FGD, ensure that all participants' voices are heard. If a participant is not speaking, then nudge them to do so – ask their opinion. If a participant is speaking too much or dominating the group, ensure that you restore balance in the group. Remember, even though I have advised you to be a facilitator for the FGD, do not be afraid to be a badass if one participant is taking over the discussion. There can be only one villain in the FGD, and that is you (whenever need be). Make it a safe space for all the participants and ensure that everyone gets the space and time to voice their opinions. Conversely, do not be afraid to take away space from few participants if they are dominating and not hearing the other participants' points of view. However, while doing this, ensure that the participant does not feel excluded from the group – bring them back into the discussion after a while. Whenever I have been in a situation where a participant dominates the group, I do not tell them anything directly, instead, I avoid them for some time and give my attention to other participants who have not been able to speak. I point towards a participant who has been quiet and ask them their opinion even when the dominating participant continues to speak. If they still continue, then I tell them that I am not able to hear the other participants' response. Try not to tell any participant that they need to shut up, instead ask the other participants to speak up.

If a few participants have a difference in opinion and get into a debate, which, after a point, seems like a fight of egos, feel free to break the conversation politely and remind both of them that there are no right or wrong answers and that both opinions are fine in their place.

Note: Just like the list of questions you want to ask the participants during interviews is known as an Interview Schedule, the list of questions that you want to ask the participants during an FGD is known as a Discussion Guide.

How to conduct interviews and FGDs like a pro: Here are some suggestions on conducting interviews like a pro. These are just advice and not rules that you have to follow. These have helped me to conduct superb interviews & FGDs, and I hope that they help you too.

- **Creating a safe space**: You can connect with your participants on a deeper level if the participants believe that they are in a safe space. They will not be afraid to share their experiences, and you will not be afraid to ask frank questions. There are two elements of creating a safe space – physical and mental.

  Physical space: Choose a place for an interview where the participant feels comfortable sharing their experiences. I prefer semi-formal cafés, which are not over crowded. While conducting market research interviews, you may not have a say in the space where the interview is conducted. Still, ensure that the location is easily accessible through local transport, and the space has basic amenities such as a clean washroom, drinking water, restaurants nearby (in case you would want to order food for yourself or the participant), and a comfortable seating arrangement. Many interviews in the post-pandemic world are conducted remotely (virtually). Give the participants instructions that will help them transform their own space into a safe space such as being in a place where other family members are not around, and there is no disturbance and distraction. Not all the participants will have a personal space at home (personal space is still a luxury for many individuals). In case you have a participant that does not have access to personal space, ask them if there is any time during the day where they could be alone and conduct the interview as per their preferred time. You may even organise a space near their home where they can talk to you freely. Always ask the participants if they would need your help with anything related to the interview. This could be any assistance before, during, or after the interview is conducted.

Mental space: You would need to ensure that the participants are in a space where they can freely share and be authentic. The simplest way of doing this is to communicate with the participants that they are in a safe space – that there are no judgements, no right or wrong answers. Take the initiative to talk to your participants. Compliment them. Buy them a cup of coffee, tea, or offer water. Smile. Introduce yourself – not just as a researcher but also as a human being. Many times, while conducting FDGs and interviews with mothers and homemakers, I ask them how their day is like on a busy day during the warm-up.

Mothers are generally the first ones to wake up and ensure that the entire family gets going. Due to patriarchal influence, the primary gender role of mothers in many societies is still nurturing and taking care of their families. When they share that they get up early in the morning, I tell them how I regularly fail to wake up to my alarm and that I always struggle to wake up early (true story). When I share how I fail at a thing that they have to do every day, they start seeing me as a human. I am a person who is not perfect. **Self-deprecation works well to create a rapport with your participants during the initial stages. It** generates empathy, and you come across as more of a human. While interacting with your participants, take care of the smaller things, and the bigger things will fall into place, and, before you realise, you would be engrossed in an interesting conversation.

- **On judgement and trusting your participants:** It is difficult to not be judgemental. It is only human to judge, but, as researchers, try to understand where they are coming from and how you can address them. If you sense a judgement, then keep a mental note of it and revisit it later to try and understand its root cause. The first step of addressing judgement is by knowing when you are judgemental. If you successfully identify your judgement, let it not show in your body language. Even when you think that you have control over your judgement, it may be reflected in your body language. Try and be aware of not just your thoughts but also of your body language. Doing this will help you to not jinx the data collection process. Remember that the interviews and FGDs are not about you but the participants. Being present to yourself, thoughts, and body language will help you maintain a safe space.

A common reason for the researcher to be judgemental is suspecting that the participant is not telling the truth. Actively listen to their stories and experiences even when you think that the participant is exaggerating or lying. Know that your thoughts on the participants' stories being true or not are just your perceptions and not the reality. During the research, you may even decide to counter-question or re-question to have clarity on what the participant is sharing with you. However, ensure that this does not transform the interview into an interrogation. When you feel that the participant is not sharing their true experiences, park the thought aside until the interview is over. Once you have time to reflect, ask yourself why you felt that way. If you still cannot trust or believe the experiences of the participant, conduct more interviews. See if similar experiences come up while interacting with other participants. If at all you still feel that a participant has not been truthful, instead of labelling their experiences and stories as a lie, maybe call it an 'outlier'. **Know that there is a huge difference between calling someone a**

liar as compared to calling someone an outlier. Try to understand from previous literature or through different tools about the reasons and situations when participants refrain from sharing their true experiences. As the last step to address this issue, you may also choose to exclude the participant's voice but have strong reasons if you are taking this step.

Section 3 – Observations

Remember the exercise on observation in Chapter 1 (Exercise 1.5: I was only observing)? All living humans observe – the act of observing is like that of breathing or sleeping. You have been doing observations since the day you were born – observing to make sense of this world. In the first chapter of this book, we have learnt a few ways to keep our observations scientific. The steps are simple – first, just observe and have a thick description of the observation. Try not to attach interpretations immediately. This will limit your ability to see multiple, varied, and deeper interpretations. Although all of us observe, we are not mindful or 'present' while making these observations. As researchers, you have to be present enough to keep your interpretations, perceptions, and judgements aside while observing. Attempt to record the stimulus in the external environment that while being aware that we are also a part of that environment. Observe not just what is happening outside of you but also what you are feeling inside. The best way to master observation is to do more and more of them. Observations can be classified into two categories: participatory and non-participatory. Let us understand what they mean and how they are different.

Participatory observation is a tool of data collection where the researcher is part of the community/environment and actively participates in it. Here, active participation means that the researcher is interacting with the community and taking part in the routine rituals conducted by the community. Participatory observations are a primary tool while conducting ethnographic studies as it requires the researcher to stay with the community. While doing participatory observations, the researcher has greater influence over the behaviour and action of the community when compared to non-participatory observation as they are interacting and involved with the community.

Non-participatory observation is when the researcher collects data on a community/environment/behaviour but from a distance. While doing non-participatory observations, the researcher does not interact with the community or individuals being observed. Hence, the researcher has limited to no influence over the community while collecting data. A good non-participatory observation is when the participants forget that they are being observed by the researcher.

In both the observation techniques (participatory and non-participatory), the community may or may not be aware of the researcher's identity. So, any of these observation techniques could be covert or overt (concepts covered in Chapter 7). However, the chances of a non-participatory observation being covert are much higher as the researcher would want to observe the real behaviour of the participants. Non-participatory observation is also commonly used as a tool in experimental social sciences research.

Participatory observation is commonly referred to as 'fly in the soup', and non-participatory observation is referred to as 'fly on the wall' in market research. However, I do not agree with these terms as it assumes the researcher to be an outsider (referred to as a fly). We have seen that the researcher may not always be an outsider. But you get the gist – 'fly in the soup' is when the researcher is in action, whereas 'fly on the wall' is when they are observing from a distance.

Exercise 5.2: Ethics of observations

Should the researcher inform the community/individuals being observed that they are being observed? How would knowing or not knowing the researcher's real identity impact the behaviour of the community/individuals?

To be a better researcher, do more and more observations. Study the facial expressions and body language of people. People can hide their feelings by not being vocal about them, but it is challenging to control one's body language. Study people in public spaces and keep a note of your observations in a diary. Try to do both participatory and non-participatory observations. With due permission, you may also conduct observations in private spaces. Be creative when and how you make observations. One of the students I was mentoring for fieldwork conducted non-participatory observations to understand the relationship between the employees who were part of the labour union and the organisation's management. She conducted these observations primarily in the formal meetings between the union leaders/members and the management. Initially, the employees were conscious of her presence, but they forgot that she was observing as time passed.

Section 4 – Diary Study

When the researcher needs to collect data from the participants on a regular interval and for a longer time, they use diary studies as a data collection tool. The researcher sends areas or questions to the participants at regular intervals. The researcher may give the participants the freedom of recording as per their convenience (but this approach will work only when the participant is either self-motivated to record regularly or a good incentive is provided to keep them motivated). In recent times, some researchers are gamifying the process – all participants can view the number of entries made by other participants and prices may be awarded to those who have been most regular or have more entries. There are advantages and disadvantages of taking this approach, and how a researcher needs to influence the participants to regularly participate can be decided depending on the sensitivity and objective of the research. Suppose data is to be recorded by participants with chronic illnesses or by pregnant women. In that case, a forced approach of a number of entries might not be an empathic approach. The researcher may give physical notebooks or diaries to the participants or ask them to record data in a virtual diary. Further, the data may be entered in a written format, or as videos or voice notes. The place (physical or virtual) and the format for recording the data (written, video, or audio) are to be decided by the researcher after considering the participants' convenience. The researcher can even give multiple options for recording the data and allow the participants to choose whatever they are most comfortable with. For instance, the data may be thicker when the participant is recording their voice as compared to when they are writing their entry. We speak at a much faster rate, and speaking is easier for most as compared to expressing ourselves when we write. The researcher should also consider factors such as age, native language, and education level before deciding on how the data is to be recorded.

Since data is collected and recorded for a long time, ensure you have taken enough steps to maintain the privacy of data and the participants' identity. (More on this in Chapter 7.)

Section 5 – Interpretation of Drawings, Pictures, and Photos

In the past few years, the use of creative tools has increased for data collection in qualitative research. One such tool is the interpretation of drawings, pictures, photos, and even videos. Let us understand some of these creative tools with examples. If, as a researcher, you want to understand the concept of family from children under 10 years of age, then, using only conventional tools may not lead to thick data. You may conduct interviews or FGDs with these children, but they may not be able to express themselves as their language is not entirely developed. Hence, you might consider a drawing activity. In this activity, you can tell them to draw whatever comes to their minds when they think of the word 'family'. Once the children are done, you can ask them to explain what they have drawn. This will help you better understand what family means for children as they may express themselves better through drawings. However, art-based research is not just used with children – it can be a great tool of data collection for adults. Let us assume that you want to research unpaid domestic work. As a part of your research, one of the cohorts you are to interact with is housewives. Now, you give all your participants (housewives) a camera or ask them to use their phones to take pictures of their day. They click photos whenever they want – of things that make them happy or the tasks that they do not like – anything that they want to share from their lives. After a week, you meet them to see the photos. Instead of asking questions about their lives from an interview schedule or conducting an FGD, just ask them to explain the meanings associated with these photos. Why have they clicked the photos that they have clicked? What emotions are attached to those photos? The participants will first explain to you the meanings attached to those photos. Then, later, you can analyse and derive interpretations out of the data. This method will be good with adults, especially when the researcher does not want predetermined areas of questioning and wants the participants to lead them through the research themes.

We have covered the major tools that are used in qualitative research (a few new and less used tools as well). You may come across various other tools that are used for collecting data in qualitative research. Who knows – someday even you may introduce newer tools and ways of collecting data in qualitative research! Now, let us go to the next chapter on analysing qualitative data.

CHAPTER 6
DATA ANALYSIS IN QUALITATIVE RESEARCH

You might be gearing up to analyse the data after completing the data collection process using various tools discussed in the last chapter. Well, in qualitative research, the data analysis process does not always follow the data collection process – many times, the researcher has to do elementary data analysis while collecting data in the field. Imagine that you are doing an ethnographic study and you have spent two years understanding a community. If you wait till your fieldwork is complete to begin recording and analysing the data, you may not even remember most of your observations. The longer the fieldwork or data collection process, the sooner you need to record, transcribe and analyse the data. Often, even during qualitative market research, I ensure that the recordings from the field are immediately transcribed so that there is not a lot of gap between the fieldwork and the analysis as I want my experiences and memories from the field to remain fresh when I analyse the data. You may also maintain a summary of daily observations and findings (for the days you have to do fieldwork). If you end up in a job that requires you to do qualitative research, you may have to share these regular summaries (commonly referred to as top lines) with the client.

Doing elementary/initial coding (or data analysis) while on the field also enables me to make necessary changes in questioning and focus areas over the period of the research. Of course, you should also keep time for data analysis after the field work is completed.

Steps in data analysis in qualitative research:

The steps of analysing qualitative data can be classified into four broad categories:

a) Coding
b) Categorisation
c) Thematic representation/analysis
d) Theorisation

Very few qualitative researchers cover all four stages of data analysis. Most of the time, the researcher would stop at the thematic representation of the data simply because theorisation may not be an objective of the research. It may also happen that the researcher does not plan to propose theories but may end up proposing a theory or an idea that has the potential of being a theory. Let us understand the data analysis process in detail.

Data analysis and coding in qualitative research: Do not worry – we are not talking about coding as a computer language. 'Coding' in qualitative research is the step of doing data analysis. Basically, coding is done to summarise, categorise, and capture the essence of the data in a shorter form. Let us say that you have collected data through various tools such as interviews, FGDs, and observations. You have put in a lot of effort to ensure that the data is thick. Towards the end of the research, you realise that you have pages and pages of data, and you do not know where and how to start analysing it. Given the effort you have put into the data collection process, you do not want to lose any important data while analysing. After all, what is the point of having a thick description and detailed data if you are not able to capture and make sense of it during analysis? This is where coding helps.

But what is coding? Let us try and understand coding with an example from our everyday lives. (Do not take this example literally, this is just to explain the nature of coding.) You must have visited a supermarket and before going there, you might have prepared a list of things that you need to buy. This list helps us remember what we need to buy. However, there are times when we might not prepare a shopping list – when there are lesser items to buy, or you want to visit the supermarket for window shopping, or if you have a great memory! Consider this list similar to an interview schedule or a discussion guide. When you meet participants, there are certain questions or areas that you would want to explore with them. However, there might also be times when you would not prepare an interview schedule or a discussion guide – if you want to keep the data collection process exploratory and free-flowing. So, you enter the supermarket with or without the list (depending on your need and context).

The supermarket, however, is huge and stocks thousands of products – how would you know where to find the products you need? If you would have noticed, the supermarket is divided into different sections or departments – they may be called meat, produce, organic, beauty and health, home products, and so on. Each section is further divided into sub-sections. For instance, meat would have sub-sections such as processed and unprocessed, branded and unbranded, organic, local or imported, or, at the very least, there will be classifications based on the type of meat (chicken, fish, beef, etc.). Further, note that different types of meat are assigned different shelves of the cold storage section. You may have noticed that these products will be segregated based on some commonality. But, how does it help you? The summarisation and categorisation of these products make it easy for the buyer to find, compare, and select the right products.

Drawing parallels to the example shared above, we already know that your interview schedule or discussion guide is like your shopping list. You make them so that you do not forget any important area to be covered in the research. You finalise a supermarket where you will find all or most of the products required. This process is similar to finding the participants for your research – you ensure that the participants selected help you in achieving the objective of the research. You know that the supermarket has a lot of products to offer and you are only interested in buying products off your list and have no intention of buying the entire supermarket. Even if you are window shopping, you may buy a lot of products but you will not buy the entire supermarket. This is similar to your data collection process with the participants. You will have your probe areas and ask questions accordingly or you may do an exploratory free-flowing conversation (like window shopping) or you may just do observations in a community (like people-watching in the supermarket). You will aim to capture data in as much detail as possible, and, over a period of time, you will have a lot of data from multiple participants. To make sense of this huge data set and to easily find the relevant data, you need to start coding. The process of coding would lead to breaking the data set into different categories and segments (also known as themes and sub-themes in qualitative research). Remember that coding, as a process, is similar to the process of categorising, segregating, and arranging products in different sections and departments in the supermarket.

I know this is a naïve way of explaining the process and that I have compared participants (humans) to supermarkets, but I hope that I was able to simplify the process of data analysis for you (and that you are not judging me for giving this lame analogy).

Coding is the process of choosing, separating, and systematically arranging data – through the technique of labelling – with the ultimate goal of having better and more meaningful interpretations.

You will code the data for yourself – so that you have better interpretations and make the most of the data while remaining grounded in it. The world will mostly be interested in your research findings/interpretations. Just because you are coding the data for yourself, it does not mean that you can afford to not be rigorous. Spend time while coding the data and re-code it to gain more perspectives, thoughts, and questions so as to provide explanations and support your interpretations. Be creative with the way you code. Come up with your own categories, terminologies, use colours, or even movie titles to code your data. Explore the process, have fun while coding, and, soon, you will find a way that suits you the most. Remember that the objective of coding is to help yourself with the interpretation of data.

I have observed that many researchers, especially in the industry, ignore the process of coding. They write the insights primarily based on either their memory or their pre-decided themes of the research and then attempt to support these points with verbatims. Very few researchers code the entire data set. I have worked in some research roles and have even witnessed that many qualitative researchers do not know how to code. I have seen that the process of coding the qualitative data is taken more seriously in academia as compared to the industry.

Before we understand the different types of coding, here are few important points to remember:

- Code rigorously. Code and then re-code the same data. You will have to do multiple rounds of coding.
- While assigning a specific code to the data, ask yourself why you have coded the way you have, and if there could be other/multiple codes for the

same data points. In case you feel that a data point will have multiple codes, write all the codes.

- Keep your codes small – preferably not more than four words. Your data is already vast, you do not need long codes (avoid codes in the form of sentences as they might complicate things further).

- Coding is an interpretive and subjective act. So, whatever you code is ultimately your views and perceptions of the meaning attached to the data.

- Due to the subjective nature of coding, different people will code the same data differently. So, do not be surprised if two people come up with different codes for the same data set. Whenever possible, use this to your advantage. Ask another researcher, colleague, or friend to code the same data. Then, discuss the similarities and differences in the two sets of code. Remember that you are not doing this exercise to prove that your codes are better but to understand various meanings attached to the same data by different individuals. (You are lucky if you have a friend or colleague who agrees to help.)

- What could be coded? Well, any data could be coded. What is 'data' in qualitative research? It could be transcripts from interviews or FGDs, field notes from observations, letters, pictures, paintings, videos, diaries, text in any form, song lyrics – you get the drift (any information that the researcher believes to be beneficial, irrespective of the source, given the research objective and questions).

Types of Coding:

Classification based on the phase when coding is conducted:

Initial/Open Coding: Coding conducted during the initial phase of data analysis is known as initial or open coding. During initial coding, the researcher moves and codes quickly through the data.

Whenever you are doing initial coding:

- Let the codes emerge from the data – do not judge or doubt yourself with the codes
- Keep the codes short and simple
- Look out for action verbs (mental and physical actions) and code them

Always conduct the initial coding; once the initial coding is done, you can choose a specific type of coding for later stages of the analysis.

Axial & Focused/Selective Coding: Both Axial and Focused/Selective Coding are the second level of coding, i.e., conducted after the initial coding. Here, the researcher reflects more and takes time to ask themselves why they have coded what they have coded, checks if the codes from the initial coding are grounded in data, and then tries to make sense of the codes.

In axial coding, the researcher attempts to relate codes to categories and sub-categories. So, you would want to club similar kinds of codes. For example, if you are researching workplace bullying, you would want to club similar codes and assign them to categories and sub-categories after coding (remember the supermarket example).

Codes: Disturbed, Nervous, Uneasy, Tensed, Hysterical

Sub-Category 1.1: Worried (Disturbed, Nervous, Tensed)

Sub-Category 1.2: Overwhelmed (Uneasy, Hysterical)

Category 1: Anxious (Worried, Overwhelmed)

Similar to this, create various sub-categories and categories to assign and cluster the codes. You may have categories such as:

Category 2: Rejected

Sub-category 2.1: Alienated

Sub-Category 2.2: Inadequate

(Remember these sub-categories will have various codes of similar nature)

Focused/Selective coding: In selective coding, the researcher chooses a theme or a category and then only codes the data that will be a good fit under that theme. Suppose the researcher decides the theme or the category to be 'Fear and Workplace Bullying', then they will only code data that has elements of fear and workplace bullying. If the researcher comes across other themes such as 'Sadness and Workplace Bullying' they will skip those codes. They will take up codes relevant to 'Sadness and Workplace Bullying' only when they have selected that theme. Here, the focus is on coding only a particular category or theme at a time and, hence, this method of coding is also known as focused coding.

Theoretical Coding: Theoretical coding is conducted towards the end of the data analysis process. It is primarily conducted when the objective of the research is to either introduce a theory or validate an existing theory/assumption. Like the previous coding methods, the researcher arranges and categorises the codes under sub-categories, categories, and themes. However, theoretical coding goes a step ahead as it tries to view patterns and relationships within and across categories/themes. Here, the focus of the researcher is on first coding the conditions/stimuli/circumstances that the participant has been exposed to. Once this is done, the researcher codes how the participant reacted/behaved to the conditions. Finally, the researcher codes the data that shall explain the outcome of such reactions/behaviours.

Classification based on the degree of inclusion and retention of the voice of participants

In-Vivo Coding: The focus while doing in-vivo coding is to retain the terms used by the participants while coding. The researcher does not create their own codes but chooses codes from the data itself. Though this method of coding limits the researcher's ability to be creative with the way codes are assigned; however, it is considered a more humanistic approach to analysing the data.

There is no hard and fast rule that you cannot choose different types of coding while analysing the data. You may decide to use in-vivo coding only for certain sections of the data and code the other sections using different techniques.

Classification based on text segmentation:

Word-by-Word; Line-by-Line; Segment-by-Segment; Incident-by-Incident coding: The names of these coding techniques are self-explanatory. During word-by-word coding, the researcher codes each word of the text. Similarly, in line-by-line coding, the researcher will code each sentence. A uniform segment (which can be a section or paragraph of the text) can be coded via segment-by-segment coding. Similarly, in incident-by-incident coding, the researcher breaks the text into various incidents and then codes each incident.

From the four types of coding (word-by-word, line-by-line, segment-by-segment, and incident-by-incident), what you choose would depend on the nature of the text. If you are coding an ancient script, a religious script, legal text, or conducting a hermeneutic study, you may want to choose word-by-word coding. While conducting analysis in the initial stage, you may prefer line-by-line or segment-by-segment coding. If you are a new qualitative researcher, you can consider coding line-by-line as it will help you develop your style of coding through practice.

The more we code, the better we become. Let us practice coding.

Exercise 6.1: Qualitative researchers code too!

The text below is a verbatim taken from the transcript of my MPhil research. The verbatim is in a raw format (no grammatical corrections made) as I wanted to represent the voice of the participant as it is. You have

---

to code this text shared with you.

Step 1: First, read the text

Step 2: Do initial coding (move fast and let the codes emerge from the text)

Step 3: Do line-by-line coding. Ensure that every line has at least one code assigned to it. (While doing this, ask yourself why you have coded what you have coded and if other codes that can be assigned to it.)

Step 4: Try to put similar codes in categories

Step 5: Observe and interpret what comes out from these categories and sub-categories

While doing this exercise, be aware of yourself, of the things that you are feeling. If there are any strong emotions and judgement, note them down.

Text to Code

Text to code	Write your codes in this column
In the interview time, when they had seen my résumé, they knew that I had worked with LGBT group. So, they know that from my résumé. They apparently did not happen to discuss anything in the interview as such, but,	

yes when I started working, I usually started chit-chatting with my colleagues and there was a discussion about marriage and all that, and I told them that let me find a good boy and then I will marry. Then they knew about it. I mean, my colleagues with whom I worked…uh, who work with me, they were taken aback and a little hesitant. But I appreciate them, they were open about it. They wanted to know about it and they wanted to understand about it and it was completely new as they had never met a gay person and they were aware about it but they were not very well-known about it.

I remember when I told them the first time, there was silence. After a couple of minutes, they were like okay, fine, is it so. They were all trying to figure out what to say and what to ask but there was no conversation that day. The next day when I was there in the office, sitting and working, uh…they were like when yesterday you said that, we both were taken aback. And I was like "Okay, I understand, it's not something which is very new or very regular. I understand that." Then one of the colleague was – "I don't know about it but I have heard about it in Germany but I have never met a gay person who was out in the open as such," and then he started asking how is it and you know, how come I am open and out and how is life in general and all that. So, he was just trying to know and understand the whole perspective of life then that there was nothing unpleasant like that.

I don't think that coming out at the workplace

is the most easy part as such, but once I started coming out, I have been out to all in my organisations, (people) that I have worked with, and there were also some religious and fundamental organisations that I have worked with. In one such organisation, when I opened up, there were few who were absolutely supportive, and when Section 377 happened, there were people who came up to me and said that we are with you for the *Jail bharo andolan.* And the rest of the persons, like there was a retired IAS officer and he was taken aback. He was like I am not judging you and all and I don't want to be rude or judgemental on you but I absolutely don't understand these things and I find them very deviant.

There were other sorts of religious organisations that I worked with, uh, spiritual organisations. So, there was this spiritual friend, I had worked with him for some time. So when I came out to him, he was one of those who...he was quite taken aback. He was quite shocked and I had never seen him so shocked during my entire work experience with him, and then he went on and told me that I should not talk about it and how should I really hide it. Some way he was looking at me as his successor in the organisation and all and then I told him that "See I am going to be open, I am not going to remain closeted. I thought I would share it with you as I consider you my mentor." So, then he went on talking about necessities and what is required to succeed in life and all that. It was a very huge conversation and we still end up talking about it, and I shared some movies with

<table>
<tr><td>

him. So, ya, that was one tough experience for me basically because, uh…someone whom I looked up as a spiritual mentor went on talking about necessities of life which we should think beyond. However, after coming out, we still are okay but there is a guy that has come in between. He is a little bit disappointed. Yes…organisations, wherever, I am open and out. There were few religious organisations that were taken aback and all that. They have their own understanding beyond which they cannot go. Otherwise I have never had trouble coming out.

</td><td></td></tr>
</table>

Analysing and coding audio-visual data: Just like you can code the textual data, you can also code pictures, videos, and sounds. The level of detailing that you need to account for will depend on the research objective – for instance, you may choose to do frame-by-frame analysis or just give an interpretation on the broader semiotics and meanings attached with the audio-visual data.

While coding a picture or a frame, you may want to observe the colour scheme, line, shape, form, the use of space, and how they impact the meaning associated with the picture. For instance, you may want to understand how the elements in the picture/frame impact the overall meaning associated by the participants. Similarly, while evaluating and coding videos, you may want to consider coding the visual and audio data. While coding the visual data, code the setting (indoor or outdoor setting), camera (positioning and angle of the camera), and the action that is taking place in the video. Different types of shots, camera angles, settings, and actions are used by video creators to depict certain emotions or convey a specific moment in the story. For instance, a bird's-eye view shot may be used to set up a context or location (you may have seen bird's-eye view or drone shots in films used as a tool to set up a location by giving an overview). Similarly, close-range shots may be used to portray a certain emotion that the actor is depicting. If you want to take up video analysis research, do read up on the basics of cinematography and the use of cameras along with other equipment to convey a story. Do not forget to pay attention to the audio data along with the video. In audio data, focus on two elements – background music and speech. While coding the background music, consider elements such as sound, melody, and harmony. Fast-paced music can be used to depict action (remember those action movies and use of fast-paced music during an action/fight scene) while minimal to no music followed by a sudden sound can be used to induce fear (silence before a jump-scare sound effect in horror movies).

Exercise 6.2: Code that meme

Memes are funny but they also tell us a lot about the culture and society that we live in. In this exercise, I want you to do a picture analysis of memes.

Here is what you have to do.

Go to the internet and shortlist five of your favourite memes on a specific area of interest. Select any topic of your choice. It could be memes related to food, people, pets or anything that you like/dislike. Now, do a picture analysis of the meme.

First, start with observing what each of the memes made you feel and how you reacted to them when seeing them the first time. Once you have noted this, do a picture analysis of the meme. You may consider various elements of the picture such as the colour scheme, line, shape, form, and use of space in the meme. If the meme has some text, then also code the text. Code intensively. Once you have coded all five memes, categorise your codes and see if any themes emerge. :)

Remember, the more you code, the better you get at it. Try coding regularly. Code newspapers, magazines, articles, your favourite novel, comments on social media, music videos, movies, or even the profiles of people on dating apps. Have fun and be creative.

CHAPTER 7
RESEARCH ETHICS AND BEYOND

I had an opportunity to be part of a research project that was exploring the problems faced by elderly women (above 60 years of age) in the slums of Mumbai. On the first day of data collection, I reached the slum selected for the study only to realise that no one was interested in talking to me. As soon as I would say the word 'research' or 'researchers', people would either just ignore me as if I did not exist, or the more polite ones would say that they were just not interested. I initially thought that perhaps the elderly women were not comfortable talking to a man, but after spending an hour at the location, I realised that not even younger people (people who looked my age) were interested in having a conversation. I was amused and wanted to know why. After many attempts, I met a participant (a woman in her 60's) who finally agreed to talk to me. Instead of going ahead with the interview schedule, I decided to ask her:

"Why does no one here want to be a participant in the research?"

To which, the elderly woman replied, "Do you think you are the first one here making false promises? We have seen many researchers like you visiting this slum almost every other day. They just come, give us false hope, and waste our time. How has our situation changed?"

It took me some time to process this information. After talking to her more, I realised that the location was a hotspot for research. Often, researchers and students would get in touch with the community to collect data. While doing this, the researchers would tell the community that their situation would change for good if they participated in the research. But, I did not promise anything to the community. While thinking it over later, I realised that not all the researchers would have lied to the community. However, many would not have clarified the outcome of the research even after knowing the community's perception of how research projects would bring some change in their standard of living. Over time, the community had reached research fatigue and thought that there was no point in participating in further research studies. This brings us to one of the most important ethical considerations in research – honesty! (Be honest with the self, with the community, and with the readers of the research.)

As researchers, it is important to not lead the community or participants to believe something that is not true (there are some exceptions that we will talk about later in the chapter). Do not promise that the research would change lives unless it is action research funded by government bodies or institutions responsible for bringing some change post research. Even when this is the case, the researcher does not know what needs to be recommended and if the recommendations will be implemented eventually. So, in most cases, the researchers should just state the objective of the research rather than making promises of change that will take place post the research. Even when you do not promise anything to the community about the impact of the research, you must clarify if the community believes otherwise. This applies to researchers and research agencies in the industry as well. Often, agencies and researchers pitch (send a tentative proposal) to lure the clients with how their previous study/research impacted another organisation's bottom line. By doing this, they give a sense of hope to the client (especially small businesses) of getting similar results if the same researcher or agency is hired. Instead, the right approach/pitch is where the researchers or research agencies strive to identify and implement suitable research methodologies, given the organisation's situation and limitations. (Do not believe research agencies that tell you that they do not pitch or do not provide tentative proposals. A pitch or a proposal is not just a way to give a taste of the approach to problem identification and solving but is also a way to show the level of sincerity, dedication, and interest in the work. What a pitch/proposal is not – is giving solutions and recommendations to the client before embarking on the research journey. Researchers and research agencies that tell you that they do not provide a proposal or a way forward are just lazy and want you to believe in a false narrative – not having a pitch is a pitch that enables them to get away with lesser work and hiding their limitations.

Being honest with yourself: While taking any research project or choosing a research methodology, question yourself – why are you doing what you are doing? As researchers, we pose questions to individuals and communities for research but often forget to ask ourselves some basic questions. I had decided to work on the diversity and inclusion of LGBTQIA+ individuals for my PhD research, and one of the important reasons for choosing this topic was that I identified with the community. I was seeking answers to what it was like to disclose (or not disclose) non-normative gender and sexual orientation identities at the workplace. It was true that I wanted to record the voices and experiences of LGBTQIA+ individuals in their workplace, but, in the process, I wanted to find my voice and test the waters by knowing the possible social and economic implications of being out in the workplace. I had to be honest about these reasons while conducting, analysing, and writing my dissertation. It was only when I was able to be honest with myself that I could be honest to the community and the readers. This is just one example, but the researchers need to be honest with themselves at every stage of the research – first ask yourself the relevant questions before questioning a participant or a community. While questioning yourself, know that not all your answers would be rational. Also, know that you may not have answers to these questions all the time. Do not try to force rationality in your answers or judge yourself for not knowing the answers; instead, be aware of what you feel and acknowledge it.

Being honest with the readers: In my short career as a qualitative researcher, I have witnessed some instances where researchers have not been honest with the readers and/or the client that they are working with. There have been times when I have seen colleagues makeup or, at least, have suggested making up verbatim – who would take the pain of going through the transcripts again and look for specific verbatims! Me disagreeing with such suggestions has largely resulted in three outcomes – first, the colleagues avoiding to work with me in future projects; second, me getting labelled as a 'traditionalist' and an 'activist'; and third, the responsibility of finding these verbatims had been entirely given to me when it is a task that should be carried out by everyone involved in the project. Not just verbatims – there have been researchers who fabricate research findings, extrapolate sample size, and whatnot! This is not just a problem with qualitative research but the overall research paradigm. There are various reasons why I think such unethical practices take place, but one of the primary reasons is the assumption and narrative around rigour, relevance, and the impact of the research study even within the academic circle. There is so much pressure on researchers – to prove that their research is rigorous and relevant, to give 'aha' or eureka moments/findings, to become publishing machines – that they give in, thus defeating the entire purpose of researching. I have come across many students doing quantitative research who believe that their research is irrelevant if the research hypothesis is not proved. In such situations, the objective of research changes from testing the hypothesis to manipulating data so that the hypothesis is accepted. Students fail to understand that rejection of the hypothesis does not mean that their research is also rejected! Similar pressure also exists among researchers and agencies in the industry where the struggle is related to being relevant, having more retainer accounts, and earning higher profits. Often, under such pressure, the researcher in the industry tells the client what the client wants to hear rather than what should be told.

Although qualitative research has a fluid and emergent design, this fluidity should not be abused. As researchers, we should take pride in seeking and contributing to knowledge.

Overt and Covert research: We have seen the importance of honesty in research. However, from a research design perspective, there are few exceptions. To understand these exceptions, we need to understand what covert and overt studies mean. An overt study is an approach where the researcher informs the participants/community of their involvement in the study. The researcher has 'informed consent' from the participants. The researcher may use various tools such as observations (participatory or non-participatory), interviews, and discussions to collect data from the participants. Most of the research carried in academics or even in the industry are overt studies – where the participants are informed and have consented to how the data will be collected and used. In some countries (mostly while doing academic work at the doctoral level), the researcher may also be required to take clearance from the Research Ethical Committee or an Advisory Committee. These committees consist of senior academicians and researchers who help/critique the research design and methodology to ensure that research ethics are followed. Often, these committees are seen not to be in favour of covert research. Hence, many covert studies are independent research projects.

But what is covert research? Covert research is where the participants/community involved in the research are not aware that they are being studied. The researcher enters the community or has conversations with the participants while not revealing their true identity and intentions. The central argument of initiating covert research is that if participants are aware of being observed or studied, they will not behave normally. Thus, not revealing that the participants are part of the study will help the researcher capture more of the true reality. However, there may be negative implications of conducting a covert study, both for the researcher and the community/individuals, especially when the researcher plans to spend a prolonged period in the field. Imagine, as a researcher, you want to study gang activities in a neighbourhood, and you attempt to enter the gang while hiding your identity of a researcher (as you feel that you will be able to have more real data if you conceal your identity). In the first place, being accepted as a gang member would be difficult, and you may have to go through various tests to prove your loyalty to the gang, but imagine the outcome when you get accepted in the gang, and, later, the gang discovers your real identity and intentions. The repercussions can be lethal! While it is true that covert studies can help the researcher record behaviours that may not be possible through overt studies, the researcher may put themselves and, at times, even the community at grave risk, especially when the research topics are sensitive. If you ever take up a covert approach to research, evaluate if the research objectives cannot be met through an overt design and the risk and repercussions in case your identity is revealed.

There is also a possibility that a research has both covert and overt elements. In such cases, the participants/community that is being studied are aware of the researcher's identity and that they are part of the research but they may not know the true objective of the research. This happens a lot in experimental research, where the participants are aware and consent to be part of the research but are not aware of the study's real objective. Elements of both covert and overt research may also be found in ethnographic/auto-ethnographic research. For example, during ethnographic research in an organisational set-up, the researcher may take permission from the top management to go ahead with the research but may not disclose their identity to the employees/workers they may interact with and observe daily to collect authentic data. Hence, as part of the research design, the researcher may not be honest at all times with the participants. The debate on what is the right way of doing research has existed for a long time. Whatever you decide to do, remember that the participants and individuals from the community are human too and not just mere sources of data for your research. When in doubt, ask yourself, how you would feel if someone did the same thing to you and then try to step into the participants' shoes and think how they would feel. If there is still some confusion, ask these difficult questions to senior researchers from academia or the industry who you consider your mentor.

Exercise 7.1: Exploring Covert Studies

Look up three examples of covert studies online and write your reflections on them. Some of the questions you can ask yourself are: Was there any ethical concerns? Would you have done something differently? Was there any impact on the participants involved in the research?

Example 1: Name of the researcher and the research:

____

Your reflections:

Example 2: Name of the researcher and the research:

____

Your reflections:

Example 3: Name of the researcher and the research:

____

Your reflections:

Respecting privacy: Whether your research is overt or covert, as a researcher, you have to ensure that your participants' privacy is protected. A common way of doing this is either by not revealing the names or giving pseudo names to your participants. However, do remember that just non-disclosure of names or assigning pseudo names does not protect your participants' identity. You will have to revisit all the other details shared by the participants and ensure that they do not signal towards their identity. While researching sensitive issues, though, try your best to keep the identities of the participants private – know that you cannot guarantee complete privacy. Communicate to the participants that there is always a risk but you will take all the necessary actions to safeguard their identity, and the research is conducted in good faith. Your job to safeguard the privacy of the participants continues even after the research is completed. Keep a track of where and how you store the data and who can access the same. In case you have to present profiles of your participants/cohort, you can use techniques such as user personas. In case you are required to share the details of the participants as part of the research project, ensure that it is communicated well, and consent is obtained from the participant. Also, such studies (where you may have to give the details of the participants) are mostly market research studies that are not of sensitive nature.

Keep in mind that you may also have to hide the identities and names of the organisations or institutions that come up in your research unless you have formal written consent from the right authorities of those organisations. I have often noticed that when students write their dissertations, they do not disclose the name of the organisations but give enough information about the organisation for the readers to guess the name. Let us take a hypothetical example: suppose I am researching the experiences of women who have undergone sexual harassment at their workplace, and I write 'a woman working in the world's most popular online search engine company having its headquarters in California said' – here, I am giving away that the woman is working at Google! Most people would know that Google is the most popular search engine in the world and then I went ahead and mentioned that the organisation has its headquarters in California, making it evident that I am talking about Google (even when I may not have mentioned the name of the organisation). If this woman had supposedly shared some very personal experiences, by hinting at her workplace, I may end up revealing her identity. Not everyone reading this research would know the woman, but there may be a possibility that few people working at Google or whom the woman may be close with will be able to guess her identity.

While conducting my MPhil and PhD research, I met many individuals from the LGBTQIA+ community. I had to ensure that nothing I wrote hinted towards the participants' identities, as many of them had not been out in most of the spaces. Even when these individuals were not out, they trusted me and shared many personal experiences. It was (and still is a huge responsibility) for me to ensure that I protect their identities and privacy. Before the interview, I would assure the participants that I would try my best to protect their identities. I would also share with the participants that I identified with the queer community and understood that coming out is a journey that is different for each individual. This would not just put the participants at ease but also enabled them to open up to me.

However, once there was an interesting incident that is still fresh in my mind. I was to interview an individual who was out and vocal about his queer identity in most spaces of society. Before beginning the interview, I told him that I would not mention any information in the research report that would hint at his identity. He replied that I could only include his voice in my research if I mentioned his real identity. For him, coming out was about reclaiming queer identities, and it was essential for him that I mentioned his identity in the research. He explained that coming out was not easy and now that he was out, he did not want to go back in the closet.

Over the years, I have reflected on this incident many times and have thought about how, most of the time, we do not ask the participants how they want their identities to be treated in the research. As researchers, we take for granted what would be best for the participants instead of asking them and taking their suggestions on the ways to proceed with communicating their experiences, voices, and identities. Since then, I ask the participants how they would want me to proceed with the information they share with me. But, over the years, I have also realised that the participants may not understand the real implications of disclosure. When you think that your participants are not entirely aware of the impact of revealing their identities on their lives, you should not disclose their identities or give information that may signal their identity, even when they say they are okay with you doing so. I realised this while asking queer individuals questions on how they present their identities on virtual platforms. It was only when I asked questions related to coming out in virtual spaces that some queer individuals realised they may have come out indirectly and unconsciously in virtual spaces. Some of them were not ready to disclose their identities in virtual spaces and wanted to check their online footprints after being interviewed for this research. As researchers, there may be times when you would be more aware of the legal, social, cultural, political, and technological environment of the society compared to the participants. There may be times when the participants will not know which information would hint at their identity as they would be sharing all the details with you. As a researcher, it would then become your duty to make the participants aware of these aspects and also ensure that their privacy is protected/treated the way they want it to be.

I know I have talked about ensuring privacy and also giving this choice to the participants (I hope I have not confused you even more). What you do would be largely dependent on:

- The sensitivity of the research topic
- Environmental factors
- The choice of the participant of how they want their identity to be treated
- The awareness of the participant on implications of revealing their identity

There may be other factors that would define the course of action for you, but remember to always keep the participants first.

Investigating sensitive topics: There have been times when I have seen fellow researchers researching sensitive topics but not being prepared for the fieldwork. As a researcher, I feel that one can never be fully prepared for what the field has to offer. However, this should not stop the researcher from giving enough thought and time to sensitise themselves and prepare for what may come.

A researcher was researching mental health issues, and, as part of the data collection, had to interact with individuals who had faced some mental trauma. The researcher had spent some time going through literature on the topic and, to an extent, had also sensitised himself to various types of mental health issues that people face. The researcher thought that he was prepared and ready to begin the research. He started interacting with the first participant and gathering data on what the participant has to face in terms of mental health challenges. Halfway through the conversation, the participant's trauma resurfaced, followed by a panic attack. The researcher was not prepared for this and did not know how to help the participant.

Had you been doing this research, would you have done something differently to be ready for the field? (Give it some thought).

Before meeting the participants: The researcher should have consulted a mental health professional before going to the field. Further, the researcher should have also reached out to a support group or, at the very least, have the contact information of support groups that could have been shared with the participants in case there was a need. Before including any participant in the research, the researcher should have gathered data on the participant's current mental health status. This would have helped the researcher to know if the participant had recovered or was still struggling with mental health issues. The researcher could have checked with the participants if they were ready to talk about their issues, if there was something that helped the participants relax while having such difficult conversations, and the necessary steps to be taken if a bad memory was triggered.

During the research: The researcher should have used different techniques to warm up to the participants and split the data collection process with one participant over multiple sessions. The researcher could have chosen a location with which the participant was familiar and felt comfortable sharing their experiences. During the interview, the researcher could have also been more observant of any discomfort in the participant's body language.

After the research: Once the data has been collected, the researcher should assure if the participant was doing alright. The researcher needs to ensure that their separation from the participant was not abrupt, and has happened naturally over some time.

The researcher does not just have to be prepared to ensure the participants' well-being, but also their own. Social scientists such as Ken Pryce and Myrna Mack have lost their lives due to their research work. A more recent case of a social scientist being murdered while doing his fieldwork was of Giulio Regeni. Wherever you go for fieldwork, irrespective of the research being of a sensitive nature or not, ensure that you list down the following things:

- Enablers, or the factors that would help you during the research
- Roadblocks, or the probable challenges that you may encounter during the research
- Superheroes, or the people who you can call/get in touch with during emergencies (They are also people who can help you with roadblocks listed. They could be your guide, a family member, a doctor, your host, an elderly person in the community, contact from the local police or government officials that you are aware of, or any other person who is aware that you are in the field and will not hesitate if you call for help.)

Irrespective of what research you conduct, ensure that you also think about how you are going to look after yourself. Stay in touch with your supervisor or people you trust and keep them updated about how you are doing in the field. Also, take care of your diet and your overall physical and mental well-being.

Thank you for coming along on this journey with me. I hope you enjoy your research journey and take up some amazing qualitative research projects. Until next time!

CHEET SHEET

Research Tools

Interviews

a) Unstructured: Allows for most fluidity in questioning. Often has themes rather than questions

b) Semi-structured: Researcher can ask questions outside the interview schedule when required

c) Structured: Sticks to the interview schedule

Focus Group Discussion: The moderator/researcher attempts to understand a common subject or shared experience with a group of people. Researcher is also interested in the manner in which individuals in the group influence

Observations

a) Participatory: The researcher actively participates with the community/environment where research is conducted (Fly in the Soup)

b) Non-participatory: The researcher observes from a distance (Fly on the Wall)

Diary Study: Used to collect data on a regular interval and for a longer time. The participants record their experiences/opinion in a physical or digital journal.

Drawing, Pictures & Photos: Data is collected using creative tools such as drawing, pictures, photos, videos, artifacts etc.

Research Methods
Narrative Method: The researcher is interested in the voices, opinions and life stories of the participants. Primary research tool used under narrative method is interviews and FGDs

Ethnography: The researcher is interested in understanding the shared beliefs, values, language and behaviour of a community which may be distant or close to the researchers location. Primary research tool is participatory observations.
Phenomenology: When the researcher attempts to understand common meaning associated with a lived phenomenon for several individuals. Understand the universal essence of individual experiences. Attempts to answer questions such as 'What it is like' and 'How does it feel'. Primary tool of data collection is interviews.

Case Study Method: When the researcher is focusing on specific unit of analysis which can be person(s), event(s) or entity/organisation(s). Often similar to investigative journalism - where the researcher has little to no influence over the outcome. Primary tools of data collection are interviews and secondary (historical) data relevant to the case.

Grounded Theory: Used when the objective is to develop, test, validate theories in social sciences. Primary tool of data collection are unstructured and semi-structed interviews to evoke open-ended conversations. Also uses observational data.

Note:

Do not confuse research tools and research methods. Research tools are used within research methods to collect data. Multiple research tools can be used within a research method. When multiple methods are used – the research is called qualitative multi-method research. When qualitative and quantitative methodology are used in a study, it is known as mixed-method research. Interviews and observations are the most commonly used tools for collecting data in qualitative research.

INTERVIEW SCHEDULE

This is a sample interview schedule. Refer to Exercise 5.1 in 'Chapter 5', where we have discussed interview as a data collection tool in detail.

Here are a few exercises that you can do

- Conduct an interview with a pet owner using this interview schedule and reflect on your experiences.
- The interview schedule shared with you is semi-structured in nature, if you were to make this unstructured or structured, what changes would you make?

~

Please note that the 'Approx. Time' is only an estimation of time required to conduct an interview. Don't worry if you exceed the mentioned time (however ensure that a longer interview does not cause fatigue to the participant).

Areas of inquiry	Approx. Time
Area 1: Introduction and Warm Up	5 to 10 mins
Area 2: Relationship with the Pet	15 to 20 mins
Area 3: Photography/Videography Habits	10 to 15 mins
Area 4: Reaction to (current & potential) Services Offered	15 to 20 mins

Area 1: Introduction and Warm Up

The researcher/interviewer introduces themselves: Hi, my name is Kunal. I am a researcher and I love talking to people. Thank you for giving us time today. Before we start the conversations, I want to tell you to be comfortable. Let me know if you need anything at any point. This is a safe space for both of us and can express ourselves freely without thinking about what is right or wrong. If there is anything that you would want to know from me at any point in time, feel free to ask me. I may take notes while we talk – that's only because I don't want to miss on anything (I have a weak memory).

1) So, now I have given my introduction – you tell me about yourself
   a) Your name
   b) What do you do?

    c) Family members (Moderator to note if the pet comes
        without probing as a family member)
    d) How is your day like (on a busy/working day & on a
        holiday/weekend) [Interviewer to note if spending time
        with the pet comes without probing]
2) Okay, now tell me about your pet
    a) What is their name. Why did you name your pet that?
    b) Which animal family do they belong
    c) What type/breed
    d) How old are they
    e) Who takes care of the pet
    f) Your first memories of them

Area 2: Relationship with the Pet

---

3) On an average day, how much time do you spend with your
    pet? Why?
    a) What activities do your do with your pet? Why?
    b) Have you participated in any event organised specially
        organised for the pets and their owners? If yes,
        i)   Which ones?
        ii)   How did you come to know about this event?
        iii) How was the overall experience ?
        iv)   Did your pet enjoy it? Why?
4) What makes your pet happy? Why?
    a) Is there any toy/treat/food that your pet really enjoys?
        Which ones and why?
    b) What is the most beautiful memory associated with
        your pet? Why?
5) What makes your pet sad? Why?
    a) How do you solve the same?
    b) Has there been any bad instance/memory associated
        with your pet? Why?
6) Are there any fears / concerns that you have for your pet?
    Why?

7) If you were to describe your pet using three words only, what will you say? Why?

8) Suppose if your pet had to describe you in few words, what will they say about you? Why?

9) In a month, how much do you approximately spend on your pet? Can you give us a brief overview? [Interviewer to indirectly use this question further to understand behaviour on spending on indulgence and premium products pet products]

Area 3: Photography/Videography Habits

10) How often do you take photos/videos of your pet? Why?

11) When was the last time you took a picture/video of your pet? Why?

12) Why do you take/not take photos/video of their pet? [Interviewer to probe further]

13) Do you post it on social media? Why? How often?

14) Have you framed any photo of your pet?
    a) If yes, where have you kept this photo?
    b) Who clicked this photo? Why?

Area 4: Reaction to (current & potential) Services Offered

15) Have you heard of professional photography service for pets?
    a) If yes, where?
        i) Do you remember your first reactions post hearing such service?
        ii) What did you feel about the idea? Why?
        iii) Did you consider/not consider it? Why?

16) Why according to you would people get their pet photographed from a professional pet photographer?

a) Do you think that getting a professional photograph is any different from you taking the picture of your pet? Why?

17) If a professional pet photography service was available to you, would you get those services? Why?

a) If yes, then for what occasions?

b) How frequently would you like to get your pet photographed from a professional photographer? Why?

18) What will be your expectations if you avail these services? Why?

a) Would you want to have digital photos or printed photos? Why?

19) How much time will you be willing to spend on a photography session with your pet? Why?

20) What do you think of these other services/concepts? [Interviewer to have a free-flowing conversation around these services and deep dive. Interviewer to also

a) Video/Photo – a day in a life of you and your pet!

b) A music video of your pet!

c) Pet memorabilia photos – restoring or clicking photos of your pet to keep it as a memory

d) A pet portfolio/journal – get photos clicked of your pet at regular interval to record their growth

e) Training session for owners of the pet – to take great photographs from mobile or personal camera. What do you think about this?

f) Any other services that could be provided by a pet photographer? Why?

167

31 DAYS OF QUALITATIVE RESEARCH

Listed below are some important terminologies used in research and it is critical for a qualitative researcher to know them. In fact knowing these terminologies and concepts would set you apart from other qualitative researchers. Use the guided list below to jot down your understanding – be curious and find out more. You can pick up one word/terminology each day and read about them from various online and off-line sources. Dance with, romance, question or even deconstruct these words/terminologies but build a habit of reading and knowing a word every day for the next 31 days! Best of luck!

Day	Topics to Study	Your understanding and reflections
1	Abduction	
2	Artifact	

3	Clinical Research	
4	Context Analysis	
5	Convenience Sampling	
6	Conversation Analysis	
7	Deconstruction	
8	Deduction	
9	Discourse Analysis	
10	Ethnomethodology	
11	Explanatory Research	

12	Exploratory Research	
13	Feminist Research	
14	Hypothesis	
15	Induction	
16	Meta-analysis	
17	Meta-Narrative	
18	Nonprobability Sampling	
19	Observer Bias	
20	Probability Sampling	
21	Projective Technique	

22	Purposive Sampling	
23	Reflexivity	
24	Sample Size in Qualitative Research	
25	Secondary Data	
26	Social Constructionism	
27	Snowball Sampling	
28	Symbolic Interactionism	
29	Theoretical Framework	
30	Transcripts	
31	Triangulation	

About The Editor

PROGYAA DUTTA is a journalist turned copywriter. She is into every aspect of the written word – be it reporting, copywriting, editing, or scriptwriting. She has penned articles for The Hindu and Outlook Business, and willingly fried her brains to help start-ups and conglomerates with branding and advertising. She is keen on spinning stories out of eavesdropped conversations, social media posts, forgotten journals, and everything in between. An overthinker by day and writer by night, catch her on Instagram and Twitter @progyaadutta.

About The Cover Page Designer

MD ZUBAER is an interdisciplinary designer based in Bangalore, currently pursuing his masters at the National Institute of Design. He specialises in creating retail experiences and humanising brand stories. He has an intense affair with *Mishti Doi*, and all things sweet. He very elegantly speaks a word or two of French. Reach out to him on Instagram @zbrmd.

About The Author

KUMAR KUNAL JHA is a qualitative researcher with experience in social, marketing and user research projects. He is a visiting faculty for Qualitative Research Methods at the Tata Institute of Social Sciences. He is a Dalai Lama Fellow, recipient of Aon Hewitt Think Tank Research Fellowship and British Council Future Leader Connect Award. He loves writing and exploring different cultures through travel. Reach out to him on Instagram @kumarkunaljha.